Language Activity Book
Student's Edition

ECCE ROMANI

A Latin Reading Program
Second Edition

PROPERTY OF
CITY OF SALEM SCHOOLS

II-A
Home and School

Longman

CHAPTER 28

PREPARING TO GO SHOPPING

Activity 28a

Fill in the forms of the relative pronoun:

	SINGULAR		
	Masculine	Feminine	Neuter
Nominative	___	___	___
Genitive	___	___	___
Dative	___	___	___
Accusative	___	___	___
Ablative	___	___	___

	PLURAL		
Nominative	___	___	___
Genitive	___	___	___
Dative	___	___	___
Accusative	___	___	___
Ablative	___	___	___

Fill in the forms of the following nouns:

	SINGULAR				
	1st Decl.	2nd Decl. Masc.	2nd Decl. Neut.	3rd Decl. Masc./Fem.	3rd Decl. Neut.
Nominative	taberna	porcus	cisium	canis	onus
Genitive	___	___	___	___	___
Dative	___	___	___	___	___
Accusative	___	___	___	___	___
Ablative	___	___	___	___	___

	PLURAL				
Nominative	___	___	___	___	___
Genitive	___	___	___	___	___
Dative	___	___	___	___	___
Accusative	___	___	___	___	___
Ablative	___	___	___	___	___

Activity 28b

Some of the forms of the relative pronoun that you wrote in the first part of Activity 28a have endings that are the same as the endings of the 1st, 2nd, and 3rd declension nouns that you wrote in the second part of the Activity.

1. List the feminine forms of the relative pronoun that have the same endings as the corresponding forms of the 1st declension feminine noun that you wrote in Activity 28a:

   _____   _____   _____   _____   _____

2. List the masculine forms of the relative pronoun that have the same endings as the corresponding forms of the masculine 2nd declension noun that you wrote in Activity 28a:

   _____   _____   _____   _____

3. List the endings of neuter nouns of the 2nd declension that are different from the endings on the masculine 2nd declension noun that you wrote in Activity 28a:

   _____   _____   _____

4. List the neuter forms of the relative pronoun that have the same endings as the corresponding forms of the neuter 2nd declension nouns:

   _____   _____

5. List the masculine forms of the relative pronoun that have the same endings as the corresponding forms of the masculine/feminine 3rd declension noun that you wrote in Activity 28a:

   _____   _____   _____

6. The endings of neuter nouns of the 3rd declension differ in some cases from the endings of the masculine/feminine 3rd declension noun that you wrote in Activity 28a. With those differences in mind, list the neuter forms of the relative pronoun that have the same endings as neuter nouns of the 3rd declension:

   _____   _____

7. List the forms of the relative pronoun that are different from any of the corresponding forms of 1st, 2nd, and 3rd declension nouns:

Masculine	*Feminine*		*Neuter*	
_____	_____	_____	_____	
_____	_____	_____	_____	
_____	_____	_____	_____	

Activity 28c

Translate each sentence. Then explain the gender, number, and case of each relative pronoun:

1. Speculum, quod Syra nōn bene tenet, novum est.

   _____

   _____

   Gender: _____

   Number: _____

   Case: _____   **(continued)**

2. Crīnēs, quōs Phrygia neglegenter pectēbat, Aurēliam vexābant.

_____

_____

Gender: _____

Number: _____

Case: _____

3. Māter fīliam, quae iam in cubiculō suō dormit, in urbem dūcere vult.

_____

_____

Gender: _____

Number: _____

Case: _____

4. Cornēlius amīcōs, quī sunt senātōrēs Rōmānī, ad cēnam invītāvit.

_____

_____

Gender: _____

Number: _____

Case: _____

5. Mercātor, cuius taberna nōn procul abest, glīrēs optimōs vēndit.

_____

_____

Gender: _____

Number: _____

Case: _____

Activity 28d

Give two other Latin words that you have had that are related to *speculum*:

1. _____   2. _____

Give English words that are derived from:

3. neglegēns _____

4. porcus _____

5. vēndere _____

CHAPTER 29

GOING TO THE MARKET

Activity 29a

Combine the following pairs of sentences by changing the second into a relative clause and inserting it into the first sentence. In every case you will substitute a relative pronoun for the word in boldface. Your new Latin sentence should match the English translation given below. The first set is done for you:

1. Aurēliae crīnēs pulchrī erant.
   Duae ancillae **crīnēs** pectēbant.

   Aurēlia crīnēs, quōs duae ancillae pectēbant, pulchrī erant.

   Aurelia's hair, which two slave-women were combing, was pretty.

2. Mercātor glīrēs optimōs vēndere solet.
   Taberna **mercātōris** est prope Forum.

   _____

   _____

   The merchant, whose shop is near the Forum, is accustomed to selling excellent dormice.

3. Vehiculum ingēns erat.
   Onus **vehiculō** portābātur.

   _____

   _____

   The vehicle, by which the load was being carried, was huge.

4. Cornēlia poētam cōnspicit.
   Poēta versūs recitat.

   _____

   _____

   Cornelia catches sight of a poet, who is reciting verses.

5. Cornēlia lectīcam ēlegantissimam videt.
   Homō in **lectīcā** recumbit.

   _____

   _____

   Cornelia sees a very elegant litter, in which a man is reclining.

6. Homō īrātus est.
   Hominī porcus currēns nocet.

   _____

   _____

   The man, whom the running pig harms, is angry.

Activity 29b

Translate the Latin sentences into English and the English sentences into Latin:

1. Quis Aurēliae crīnēs pectēbat?

_____

2. Whose hair was the slave-woman combing?

_____

3. Porcus quīdam per viam currēbat.

_____

4. I saw a certain pig in the street.

_____

5. Cūr homō īrātus erat?

_____

6. The man was angry because he was lying in the mud.

_____

7. Quem poētam in viā vīdistī?

_____

8. I saw a certain poet reciting verses.

_____

9. Quae fēmina glīrēs emere vult?

_____

10. How angry the woman is!

_____

Activity 29c

Read the following passage and follow the instructions:

CORNĒLIA:	Quid heri fēcistī, Marce? Tē invenīre nōn potuī.
MARCUS:	Postquam surrēxī, ego et Sextus exīre cōnstituimus. Ubi in viās iimus, mīlitēs multōs vīdimus. Mīles quīdam quī nōs cōnspexit, "Unde vōs vēnistis?" rogāvit. "Nōnne pater vōs iussit domī manēre? Pater tuus, ubi vōs domī nōn invēnit, mē in urbem mīsit. Mē iussit vōs domum statim dūcere." 5
CORNĒLIA:	Quid dīxistī? Nōnne mīlitem timuistī?
MARCUS:	Ubi haec audīvī, tacuī, nam in viās exīre nōn licuit. Nōn mīlitem timuī, sed patrem. Ego domum redīre voluī, sed Sextus, "Cūr vēnistī, ignāve," inquit, "sī patrem timēs? Ego nōlō redīre," et in viam sē praecipitāvit.
CORNĒLIA:	Quid accidit? 10
MARCUS:	Mīles eum petīvit, togā arripuit. Brevī tempore nōs ad patrem dūxit. Sextus effugere nōn potuit.
CORNĒLIA:	Pūnīvitne vōs pater?
MARCUS:	Nōn est necesse id rogāre. Sedēre nōn possum.

For each of the following verbs from this story, give the prefix in its original, unchanged form, the infinitive of the simple verb from which the compound form is made, and the meaning of the verb as it is used in the story above. The first one is done for you.

	Prefix	Simple Verb (Infinitive)	Meaning
1. invenīre (line 1)	in-	venīre	to find
2. exīre (line 2)			
3. redīre (line 8)			
4. accidit (line 10)			
5. arripuit (line 11)			
6. effugere (line 12)			

Activity 29d

Give definitions of the following English words that are derived from Latin words in Chapter 29. Use an English dictionary as necessary:

1. mendicant _____

2. recumbent _____

3. definitive _____

4. libertine _____

_____

5. fumigate _____

_____

6. perfume _____

_____

CHAPTER 30 — FIRE!

Activity 30a

Answer the following questions with full sentences in Latin. Base your answers on the story at the beginning of Chapter 30.

1. Cūr "Cavē, Cornēlia!" clāmāvit Aurēlia? _____

_____

2. Cūr Cornēlia aedificium vix vidēre poterat? _____

_____

3. Unde bona ab incolīs ēiciuntur? Ubi pōnuntur ōrnāmenta? _____

_____

4. Quī quaerēbant parentēs suōs? _____

_____

5. Quid faciēbant aliī ex adstantibus? _____

_____

6. Quid dīxērunt adstantēs quī nihil faciēbant? _____

_____

7. Quem cōnspexērunt in tertiō īnsulae tabulātō? _____

_____

8. Cūr Cornēlia valdē commovētur? _____

_____

9. Quid accidit magnō fragōre? _____

_____

10. Quid aedificiī tandem manēbat? _____

_____

Activity 30b

Change each of the following verbs from active to passive voice, keeping the same person and number; then translate both verbs. The first one is done for you.

1. trahēbam   *I was dragging*

   _trahēbar_____   *I was being dragged*

2. quaerēbās   _____

   _____   _____

3. agit

_____

4. mittis

_____

5. pōnent

_____

6. tenēbis

_____

7. servātis

_____

8. commovēs

_____

9. relinquam

_____

10. cūrāmus

_____

11. audiēs

_____

12. vidēbō

_____

13. exspectābātis

_____

14. impedīs

_____

15. ferēbat

_____

16. dūcēs

_____

Activity 30c
Translate:

1. Ancillae crīnēs cūrābant. Crīnēs ab ancillīs cūrābantur. _____

_____

_____

2. Aurēlia ā Syrā vexātur. Syra Aurēliam vexat. _____

_____

3. Māter glīrēs emit. Glīrēs ā mātre emuntur. _____

_____

4. Aurēlia tē in urbem dūcet. Tū ab Aurēliā in urbem dūcēris. _____

_____

_____

5. Multī adstantēs in viīs ā nōbīs vidēbantur. Nōs multōs adstantēs in viīs vidēbāmus.

_____

_____

6. Incolae vōs ex aedificiō efferent. Vōs ex aedificiō ab incolīs efferēminī.

_____

_____

7. Illī līberī mē commovēbant. Ego ab illīs līberīs commovēbar. _____

_____

_____

8. Ego tē nōn servābō, nam ego illō incendiō terreor. Tū ā mē nōn servāberis, nam illud
incendium mē terret. _____

_____

_____

9. Nōs flammīs et fūmō paene opprimimur. Flammae et fūmus nōs paene opprimunt.

_____

_____

10. Tū ex aedificiī iānuā ā mē traheris. Ego tē ex aedificiī iānuā trahō.

_____

_____

Activity 30d
Fill in the blanks to match the English cues:

1. Aurēlia cōnspexit īnsulam _____
   _____ flammae ēmittēbantur. (from which)

2. Illud aedificium _____ Cornēlia spectat
   _____obscūrātur. (which) (by smoke)

3. Adstantēs _____ _____servāre
   nōn possunt. (these tenants)

4. Nōs omnēs flammīs mox _____ . (will be overwhelmed)

5. Aqua _____adstantēs in flammās iaciēbant incendium nōn
   extinguēbat. (which)

6. Mātrēs ab līberīs suīs _____ . (were being sought)

7. Mulierēs _____ līberōs servāre nōn possumus magnā vōce
   clāmant. (whose)

8. Mulier _____ cum līberīs est in tertiō tabulātō. (a certain)

9. _____ parvī ā mātribus _____ .
   (babies) (are carried out)

10. Glīrēs _____ ab Aurēliā _____
    optimī erunt. (which) (will be bought)

11. Ab illīs mulieribus miserīs _____ . (I am moved)

12. Mendīcus _____ pecūniam dedimus tunicam sordidam
    gerēbat. (to whom)

13. Illa cista ē _____ _____ . (the
    window) (is thrown out)

14. Incolae _____ bona sua _____
    līberōs suōs ē iānuīs efferēbant. (either...or)

15. Cūr _____ ā līberīs _____hodiē
    vidēbās?   (were you moved) (that)

16. _____ _____ ā mātribus vestrīs
    _____. (without doubt) (you will be saved)

17. Flammae ad eōs _____ advēnerant. (almost)

18. Tōtum aedificium fūmō et flammīs mox _____ . (will be
    hidden)

19. Spectāculum _____ _____
    numquam anteā vīdī. (so miserable)

20. Porcum _____ ē manibus servī effūgit
    _____ vītāvimus. (which) (with difficulty)

Activity 30e

Give the meaning of each of the following English words and give the Latin word(s) to which each English word is related:

	Latin Word(s)	*Meaning of English Word*
1. commotion	_____	_____
		_____
2. incendiary	_____	_____
3. query	_____	_____
4. oppress	_____	_____
		_____
5. incense	_____	a. (noun) _____
		_____
		b. (verb) _____
		_____
6. quest	_____	_____
7. emit	_____	_____
8. inquiry	_____	_____
		_____
9. ornament	_____	_____
		_____
10. eject	_____	_____
11. defenestration	_____	_____
		_____
12. peninsula	_____	_____
		_____
		_____

CHAPTER 31 | PSEUDOLUS

Activity 31a

Answer the following questions with full sentences in Latin. Base your answers on the story at the beginning of Chapter 31.

1. Quid audiēbātur ab eīs quī in culīnā erant?

_____

_____

2. Quid Pseudolus lanium rogāvit?

_____

3. Quantum pretium audītur?

_____

4. Habetne alius lanius in hāc viā meliōrem carnem?

_____

_____

5. Sī Pseudolus multum emet, quid accidet?

_____

_____

6. Ā quō porcus cūrābātur?

_____

7. Cui lanius porcum vēndere vult?

_____

8. Quī rēctē praedōnēs vocantur?

_____

9. Quot dēnāriīs porcus et lepus Pseudolō trāduntur?

_____

10. Quid Aurēlia in animō habet facere?

_____

_____

Activity 31b

Change each of the following present active infinitives to passive:

1. movēre _____ 3. trādere _____

2. pūnīre _____ 4. revocāre _____

In the 1st, 2nd, and 4th conjugations, the present passive infinitive is made by dropping the final _____ from the active infinitive and adding the letter _____ . In the 3rd conjugation, the present passive infinitive is made by dropping the letters _____ from the active infinitive and adding the letter _____ .

Activity 31c
Complete the following sentences with passive forms of the infinitives given in parentheses. Then translate the sentences:

1. Cornēlius raedam ē fossā _____ iussit. (extrahere)

   _____

2. Aurēlia porcum pinguem _____ volēbat. (emere)

   _____

3. Porcus ā laniō _____ nōlēbat. (capere)

   _____

4. Aurēlia Pseudolum _____ vult. (pūnīre)

   _____

5. Pseudolus in urbe _____ volēbat. (retinēre)

   _____

Activity 31d
Rewrite the following sentences, using passive forms of the verbs and making other changes as necessary. The first one is done for you.

1. Dominus saepe multās et optimās cēnās dat. *Multae et optimae cēnae ā dominō saepe*

   dantur.

   _____

2. Hodiē dominus tē ad cēnam accipiet. _____

   _____

3. Omnēs convīvae fābulās nārrābunt. _____

   _____

4. Quattuor servī Cornēlium in lectīcā portābant. _____

   _____

5. Invītābitne Cornēlius nōs ad cēnam? _____

   _____

6. Flammae incolās īnsulae opprimunt. _____

   _____

7. Iocus procāx servōs dēlectābit. _____

   _____

8. Plaustra lapidēs quadrātōs ferunt. _____

   _____

9. Tū fābulam nārrābis. _____

10. Sellae Aurēliam et Cornēliam per viās urbis portant. _____

   _____

Activity 31e

Fill in the blanks to match the English cues. Put the adjectives *ille, hic,* and *īdem* before the nouns they modify and the adjective *ipse* after the noun it modifies:

1. Mercātor leporem vēndit.

   _____ leporem vēndit. (That merchant)

   _____ leporem vēndit. (This merchant)

   _____ leporem vēndidit. (The merchant himself)

   _____ leporem alium vēndidit. (The same merchant)

2. Pseudolus laniō pecūniam trādit.

   Pseudolus _____ pecūniam trādit. (to that butcher)

   Pseudolus _____ pecūniam trādit. (to this butcher)

   Pseudolus _____ pecūniam trādit. (to the butcher himself)

   Alius servus _____ pecūniam trādidit. (to the same butcher)

3. Īra dominae erat magna.

   Īra _____ erat magna. (of that mistress)

   Īra _____ erat magna. (of this mistress)

   Īra _____ erat magna. (of the mistress herself)

   Īra _____ erat magna. (of the same mistress)

4. Pretium leporum erat octō dēnāriī.

   Pretium _____ erat octō dēnāriī. (of those hares)

   Pretium _____ erat octō dēnāriī. (of these hares)

   Pretium _____ erat octō dēnāriī. (of the hares themselves)

   Pretium _____ erat octō dēnāriī. (of the same hares)

5. Numquam Messalla ad cēnam sine clientibus venit.

   Numquam Messalla ad cēnam sine _____ venit. (those clients)

   Numquam Messalla ad cēnam sine _____ venit. (these clients)

   Numquam Messalla ad cēnam sine _____ venit. (the clients themselves)

   Numquam Messalla ad cēnam sine _____ venit. (the same clients)

Activity 31f
Translate into Latin:

1. Loud laughter was heard from the kitchen by Marcus and Sextus.

    _____

    _____

2. That merchant ordered this fat pig to be led away by Pseudolus.

    _____

    _____

3. The pig itself was being led through the door into the kitchen.

    _____

    _____

4. Cornelius himself will never order Pseudolus to be sent to the country house and farm.

    _____

    _____

5. Cornelius never invites the same guests to dinner.

    _____

    _____

Activity 31g
Give the Latin word from which each of the following English words is derived:

1. diminish _____

2. addition _____

3. gratis _____

4. precious _____

5. accept _____

6. rectitude _____

7. pasture _____

8. carnivore, carnation, carnival _____

9. predator _____

10. celebrated _____

CHAPTER 32

DINNER PREPARATIONS

Activity 32a

Change each of the following verbs from active to passive voice, keeping the same tense, person, and number; then translate both verbs. The gender of the implied subject of each verb is indicated in parentheses; use this information to determine the ending of the perfect passive participle. The first one is done for you.

1. iussit (masc. subject)   he ordered (has ordered)

   iussus est   he was ordered (has been ordered)

2. audīverat (fem. subject)

3. trāxistī (fem. subject)

4. parāvimus (masc. subject)

5. mīserō (fem. subject)

6. commōverant (neut. subject)

7. portāverit (masc. subject)

8. attulerāmus (fem. subject)

9. oppressit (neut. subject)

10. ēiēcī (masc. subject)

Activity 32b

Rewrite the following sentences using passive forms of the verb and making other changes as necessary. The first one is done for you.

1. Pseudolus porcum tulit.
   Porcus ā Pseudolō lātus est.

2. Aurēlia servōs in Forum mīserat.

3. Aurēlia fīliae, "Heri," inquit, "ego tē in urbem dūxī."

4. Servī ōva et māla comparāvērunt.

5. "Domina mē," inquit Pseudolus, "ad tabernam laniī mīsit."

(continued)

6. Crās tertiā hōrā ego glīrēs ēmerō.

_____

7. Cornēlius illōs amīcōs ad cēnam invītāverat.

_____

8. Clāmōrēs incolārum miserōrum Cornēliam terruerant.

_____

9. "Illa māter līberōs tenēns," inquiunt Aurēlia et Cornēlia, "nōs valdē commōvit."

_____

_____

10. Flammae et fūmus magnum aedificium oppressērunt.

_____

Activity 32c

Fill in the blanks to match the English cues:

1. "Ego," inquit Titus, "ad cēnam Cornēliī _____ _____ _____ . (courteously) (have been invited)

2. _____, _____, _____ in Forō _____ _____ . (eggs, apples, vegetables) (had been bought)

3. Ubi _____ in mediō trīclīniō _____ _____ , cibus ē culīnā efferētur. (table) (is placed/will have been placed)

4. Servī trēs lectōs _____ _____ posuērunt. (around the table)

5. _____ et _____ in trīclīnium ā servīs _____ _____ . (Bread) (chickens) (were brought in)

6. In pariete _____ erat pictūra _____ . (of the dining room) (very beautiful)

7. "_____ _____ in ātriō," inquiunt complūrēs ē senātōribus, "ā Cornēliō ipsō _____ _____ . (At the hour of/for dinner) (we were greeted)

8. In hāc pictūrā vidēmus _____ in _____ habitat Plūtō. (kingdom) (which)

9. _____ recumbēbant in tribus lectīs _____ in trīclīniō _____ _____ . (guests) (which) (had been placed)

10. Nōnne, ō māter, ab hīs miserīs _____ _____? (you have been moved)

Activity 32d

Translate into Latin:

(Titus, uncle of Marcus and Cornelia, has been invited to the dinner which will be given for senators by Cornelius. Titus is being prepared by his slave, Polydorus.)

POLYDORUS: A sedan-chair has been hired for you, master.

TITUS: Good! Now help me. This toga has not been placed properly. When I walk, without doubt it will fall.

POLYDORUS: In what shop was this toga bought, master? It is dirty.

TITUS: What? Dirty? The slave who bought this toga will certainly be punished. Bring me another toga at once!

(The sedan-chair which had been hired by the slave has been brought to the door.)

TITUS' WIFE: Come on, Titus. The sedan-chair is here. If you arrive late, as you well know, you will be scolded by your brother.

TITUS (who is coming out of the bedroom): Yes, I know that. I am finally ready. Find the slave who bought that dirty toga. I will punish him when I have returned.

(Titus sits in the sedan chair and is quickly carried through the streets by the slaves.)

_____
_____
_____
_____
_____
_____
_____
_____
_____
_____
_____
_____
_____
_____
_____
_____
_____
_____
_____

Activity 32e

For each italicized English word below, give the Latin word to which the English
word is related. Then complete each clause with the meaning of the English word:

Latin Word	If you are—	Meaning of the English Word
_____	1. *adducing* facts in an argument, you are	_____ _____
_____	2. *accepting* an offer, you are	_____
_____	3. *deferring* a decision, you are	_____
_____	4. making an *exception* to a rule, you are	_____ _____
_____	5. *educating* a child, you are	_____
_____	6. putting an *addition* on your house, you are	_____
_____	7. *circumventing* the law, you are	_____
_____	8. *reigning* over an empire, you are	_____
_____	9. drawing an *oval* shape, you are making a figure that is	_____

Activity 33a

Fill in the blank in each of the following sentences with the perfect passive participle of the verb in parentheses. Make the participle agree with the italicized noun in gender, case, and number. Then translate the sentence. The first one is done for you.

1. *Ōrnāmenta* ē fenestrīs _____ēiecta_____ in viam cecidērunt. (ēicere) _____The_____

   furnishings thrown from the window fell into the street.

   _____

2. Cornēlia ā *muliere* flammīs _____ valdē commovētur. (opprimere)

   _____

   _____

3. Cornēlius *senātōrēs* ad cēnam _____ cōmiter salūtābat. (invītāre)

   _____

4. *Servī* in urbem ā dominā _____ pānem et holera comparāvērunt. (mittere)

   _____

5. Aurēlia *glīrēs* ā coquō _____ dīligenter īnspicit. (parāre) _____

   _____

   _____

6. Servus *soleās* ā convīvīs _____ dīligenter custōdit. (dēpōnere)

   _____

   _____

7. Cornēlius omnibus *convīvīs* in trīclīnium _____ , "Accumbite," inquit, "in hīs lectīs." (dūcere) _____

   _____

8. Servī *porcum* ā Pseudolō _____ in trīclīnium portant. (emere)

   _____

   _____

9. *Coquus* ā Cornēliō _____ ē culīnā festīnāvit. (vocāre) _____

   _____

   _____

sēcum, *with them(selves)*

10. Convīvae in *mappīs* sēcum _____ cibum auferent. (ferre) _____

   _____

Activity 33b
Fill in the blanks to match the English cues:

1. _____ convīvae in lectīs _____ . (several) (were reclining)

2. _____ convīvārum extrā trīclīnium _____ _____ . (sandals) (were laid down)

3. Cornēlius ā Titō _____ nihil tamen dīxit. (having been annoyed)

4. Gustātiō ā _____ in _____ posita erat. (the cook) (trays)

5. Convīvae _____ _____ celeriter ēdērunt. (black olives)

6. Clientēs quoque ā Cornēliō _____ in ātriō stābant. (having been invited)

7. Omnēs convīvae porcum ā servīs _____ valdē laudāvērunt. (having been carved)

8. Circum porcum erant _____ glīrēs quōs Aurēlia ēmerat. (the same)

9. Clientibus _____ pullōrum data sunt, sed _____ convīvīs dē porcō datum est. (scraps) (the rest of)

10. Cornēlius _____ Titō esse _____ . (very angry) (ought)

11. Titus _____ cum clientibus, " _____ !" clāmāvit. (together) ("Hurray!")

12. _____ _____ in trīclīnium portātae sunt in quibus fuērunt _____ et _____ . (the desert) (grapes) (pears)

13. Post cēnam clientēs cibum ā convīvīs nōn _____ in mappīs auferent. (having been eaten).

14. Cornēlius _____ clientēs ad omnēs cēnās invītāre _____ . (the same) (was accustomed)

15. Convīvae cēnā _____ coquum laudāvērunt. (having been delighted)

Activity 33c
Rewrite each of the following sentences, dropping the relative pronoun and replacing the other words in bold type with a perfect passive participle and an ablative with *ā/ab*. Make the participle agree in gender, case, and number with the italicized noun. Then translate the new sentences. The first one is done for you.

1. *Cornēlia* **quam māter vocāverat**, in cubiculum festīnāvit.

   Cornēlia ā mātre vocāta in cubiculum festīnāvit. _____

   When she was called by her mother, Cornelia hurried into the bedroom. _____

2. *Flammae*, **quās Cornēlia vīderat**, multōs incolās oppressērunt.

   _____

   _____

3. *Pseudolus* *pretium*, **quod lanius petīvit**, dare nōn vult.

   _____

   _____ (continued)

4. *Fābula*, **quam Syrus nārrāverat**, puerōs valdē dēlectāvit.

_____

5. Servī *cibōs*, **quōs convīvae relīquērunt**, celeriter auferunt.

_____

6. *Coquus*, **quem Cornēlius laudāverat**, in culīnam laetus rediit.

_____

Activity 33d
Translate into Latin:

1. The guests invited to dinner were waiting for Cornelius in the atrium.

_____

_____

2. Soon Cornelius entered and greeted all the guests with a smile.

_____

_____

3. Having been led into the dining room by slaves, the guests reclined on couches.

_____

_____

4. The slave-women ordered by Cornelius carried water to the guests.

_____

_____

5. The guests washed their hands.

_____

6. The hors d'oeuvres placed on the table delighted the clients.

_____

7. The rest of the guests praised the dormice bought by Aurelia herself.

_____

_____

8. The dinner prepared by Cornelius' cook was praised by everyone.

_____

_____

9. The clients were happy because they were allowed to take scraps of chicken home to their children.

_____

_____

Activity 33e

Give the Latin compound verb (infinitive form) to which each of the following
English words is related and give the meaning of the compound verb. For each
English word write a sentence that illustrates the meaning of the word.

	Latin Compound Verb	*Meaning of the Latin Verb*
1. incumbent	_____	_____
	_____	
	_____	
2. remiss	_____	_____
	_____	
	_____	
3. elated	_____	_____
	_____	
	_____	
4. emotion	_____	_____
	_____	
	_____	
5. prevent	_____	_____
	_____	
	_____	

NOUNS

1st Declension

anima, -ae, f., *soul, "heart"*
convīva, -ae, f., *guest (at a banquet)*
fenestra, -ae, f., *window*
flamma, -ae, f., *flame*
incola, -ae, m./f., *inhabitant, tenant*
īnsula, -ae, f., *island, apartment building*
lūna, -ae, f., *moon*
memoria, -ae, f., *memory*
mēnsa, -ae, f., *table*
  secundae mēnsae, -ārum, f. pl., *second course, dessert*
neglegentia, -ae, f., *carelessness*
olīva, -ae, f., *olive*
perna, -ae, f., *ham*
pestilentia, -ae, f., *plague*
popīna, -ae, f., *eating-house, bar*
rixa, -ae, f., *quarrel*
sella, -ae, f., *sedan chair, seat, chair*
solea, -ae, f., *sandal*
stēla, -ae, f., *tombstone*
umbra, -ae, f., *shadow, shade (of the dead)*
ūva, -ae, f., *grape, bunch of grapes*

2nd Declension

asparagus, -ī, m., *asparagus*
bōlētus, -ī, m., *mushroom*
cachinnus, -ī, m., *laughter*
candēlābrum, -ī, n., *candelabrum, lamp-stand*
coquus, -ī, m., *cook*
dēnārius, -ī, m., *denarius (silver coin)*
dī (nom. pl. of deus)
dubium, -ī, n., *doubt*
ferculum, -ī, n., *dish, tray*
frustum, -ī, n., *scrap*
fūmus, -ī, m., *smoke*
incendium, -ī, n., *fire*
īnferī, -ōrum, m. pl., *the underworld*

iussa, -ōrum, n. pl., *commands, orders*
lanius, -ī, m., *butcher*
lībertus, -ī, m., *freedman*
locus, -ī, m., *place*
mālum, -ī, n., *apple*
medicus, -ī, m., *doctor*
mendīcus, -ī, m., *beggar*
mulsum, -ī, n., *wine sweetened with honey*
nāsus, -ī, m., *nose*
oleum, -ī, n., *oil*
ōrnāmentum, -ī, n., *decoration;* pl., *furnishings*
ōvum, -ī, n., *egg*
pallium, -ī, n., *cloak*
passum, -ī, n., *raisin-wine*
pirum, -ī, n., *pear*
pōculum, -ī, n., *cup, goblet*
porcus, -ī, m., *pig*
pretium, -ī, n., *price*
pullus, -ī, m., *chicken*
rēgnum, -ī, n., *kingdom*
spectāculum, -ī, n., *sight, spectacle*
speculum, -ī, n., *mirror*
strātum, -ī, n., *sheet, covering*
tabulātum, -ī, n., *story, floor*
trīclīnium, -ī, n., *dining room*
vestīmentum, -ī, n., *clothing;* pl., *clothes*

3rd Declension

adstantēs, adstantium, m. pl., *bystanders*
carō, carnis, f., *meat, flesh*
crīnēs, crīnium, m. pl., *hair*
fīnis, fīnis, gen. pl., fīnium, m., *end*
glīs, glīris, gen. pl., glīrium, m., *dormouse*
gustātiō, gustātiōnis, f., *hors d'oeuvre, first course*
holus, holeris, n., *vegetable*
ignis, ignis, gen. pl., ignium, m., *fire*
īnfāns, īnfantis, m./f., *infant, young child*

lepus, leporis, m., *hare*
liquāmen, liquāminis, n., *garum (a sauce made from fish, used to season food)*
pānis, pānis, gen. pl., pānium, m., *bread*
pariēs, parietis, m., *wall (of a house or room)*
pecus, pecoris, n., *livestock, sheep, and cattle*
sanguis, sanguinis, m., *blood*
versipellis, versipellis, gen. pl., versipellium, m., *werewolf*
vestis, vestis, gen. pl., vestium, f., *clothing, garment*
vīs, acc., vim, abl., vī, f., *force, amount*

4th Declension

versus, -ūs, m., *verse, line (of poetry)*

ADJECTIVES

1st and 2nd Declension

aspersus, -a, -um, *sprinkled*
celerrimus, -a, -um, *fastest, very fast*
cēterī, -ae, -a, *the rest, the others*
ēlegantissimus, -a, -um, *most elegant*
fidēlissimus, -a, -um, *most faithful*
īnfirmus, -a, -um, *weak, shaky, frail*
īrātissimus, -a, -um, *most/very angry*
lapideus, -a, -um, *of stone, stony*
multus, -a, -um, *much*
niger, nigra, nigrum, *black*
nōtus, -a, -um, *known*
optimus, -a, -um, *best, very good, excellent*
ōrnātus, -a, -um, *decorated*
parvus, -a, -um, *small*
proximus, -a, -um, *nearby*
pulcher, pulchra, pulchrum, *beautiful, pretty, handsome*

pulcherrimus, -a, -um, *most/very beautiful*
situs, -a, -um, *located, situated*
urbānus, -a, -um, *of the city/town*
vexātus, -a, -um, *annoyed*

3rd Declension
celeber, celebris, celebre, *famous*
celer, celeris, celere, *swift*
complūrēs, -ēs, -a, *several*
ēlegāns, ēlegantis, *elegant, tasteful*
fidēlis, -is, -e, *faithful*
miserābilis, -is, -e, *miserable, wretched*
neglegēns, neglegentis, *careless*
pinguis, -is, -e, *fat, rich*
procāx, procācis, *insolent;* as slang, *pushy*

DEMONSTRATIVE ADJECTIVES AND PRONOUNS

hic, haec, hoc, *this, the latter*
īdem, eadem, idem, *the same*
ille, illa, illud, *that; he, she, it; the former; that famous*
ipse, ipsa, ipsum, *himself, herself, itself, themselves, very*
is, ea, id, *he, she, it; this, that*

VERBS

1st Conjugation
comparō, -āre, -āvī, -ātus, *to buy, obtain, get ready*
concursō, -āre, -āvī, -ātus, *to run to and fro, run about*
dēdicō, -āre, -āvī, -ātus, *to dedicate*
dēlectō, -āre, -āvī, -ātus, *to delight, amuse*
excūsō, -āre, -āvī, -ātus, *to forgive, excuse*
  sē excūsāre, *to apologize*
invītō, -āre, -āvī, -ātus, *to invite*
numerō, -āre, -āvī, -ātus, *to count*
obscūrō, -āre, -āvī, -ātus, *to hide*

recitō, -āre, -āvī, -ātus, *to read aloud, recite*
ululō, -āre, -āvī, –ātus, *to howl*
vocō, -āre, -āvī, -ātus, *to call, invite*
vulnerō, -āre, -āvī, -ātus, *to wound*

2nd Conjugation
careō, carēre, caruī, caritūrus + abl., *to need, lack*
commoveō, commovēre, commōvī, commōtus, *to move, upset*
compleō, complēre, complēvī, complētus, *to fill*
dērīdeō, dērīdēre, dērīsī, dērīsus, *to laugh at, get the last laugh*
retineō, retinēre, retinuī, retentus, *to hold back, keep*

3rd Conjugation
accumbō, accumbere, accubuī, accubitūrus, *to recline (at table)*
addō, addere, addidī, additus, *to add*
bibō, bibere, bibī, *to drink*
coquō, coquere, coxī, coctus, *t cook*
dēpōnō, dēpōnere, dēposuī, dēpositus, *to lay down, put aside, set down*
effundō, effundere, effūdī, effūsus, *to pour out;* pass., *to spill*
ēmittō, ēmittere, ēmīsī, ēmissus, *to send out*
ēvertō, ēvertere, ēvertī, ēversus, *to overturn, upset*
exstinguō, exstinguere, exstīnxī, exstīnctus, *to put out, extinguish*
exuō, exuere, exuī, exūtus, *to take off*
irrumpō, irrumpere, irrūpī, irruptus, *to burst in*
minuō, minuere, minuī, minūtus, *to lessen, reduce, decrease*
opprimō, opprimere, oppressī, oppressus, *to overwhelm*

pāscō, pāscere, pāvī, pāstus, *to feed, pasture*
pectō, pectere, pexī, pexus, *to comb*
prōcēdō, prōcēdere, prōcessī, prōcessūrus, *to go forward*
quaerō, quaerere, quaesīvī, quaesītus, *to seek, look for, ask (for)*
recumbō, recumbere, recubuī, *to recline, lie down*
reprehendō, reprehendere, reprehendī, reprehēnsus, *to blame, scold*
rumpō, rumpere, rūpī, ruptus, *to burst*
scindō, scindere, scidī, scissus, *to cut, split, carve*
vēndō, vēndere, vēndidī, vēnditus, *to sell*

3rd Conjugation -iō
accipiō, accipere, accēpī, acceptus, *to receive, get, welcome*
aufugiō, aufugere, aufūgī, *to run away, escape*
dēiciō, dēicere, dēiēcī, dēiectus, *to throw down;* pass., *to fall*
ēiciō, ēicere, ēiēcī, ēiectus, *to throw out, wash overboard*
reficiō, reficere, refēcī, refectus, *to remake, redo, restore*

4th Conjugation
grunniō, -īre, *to grunt*

Irregular
afferō, afferre, attulī, allātus, *to bring, bring to, bring in*
auferō, auferre, abstulī, ablātus, *to carry away, take away*
edō, ēsse, ēdī, ēsus, *to eat*
efferō, efferre, extulī, ēlātus, *to carry out, bring out*
ineō, inīre, iniī, initus, *to go into, enter*

PRONOUNS

See Demonstrative Adjectives and Pronouns above

quī, quae, quod, *who, which, that*

PREPOSITIONS

ā or **ab** + abl., *from, by*
circum + acc., *around*
inter + acc., *between, among*

ADVERBS

cōmiter, *courteously, graciously, in a friendly way*
forte, *by chance*
grātīs, *free, for nothing*
immō, *rather, on the contrary*
magnopere, *greatly*
merīdiē, *at noon*
neglegenter, *carelessly*
paene, *almost*
posteā, *afterwards*
prius, *earlier*

quidem, *indeed*
rectē, *rightly, properly*
tam, *so*
umquam, *ever*
ūnā, *together*
vērō, *truly, really, indeed*

CONJUNCTIONS

ac, *and*
autem, *however, but, moreover*
dōnec, *until*
quod, *because;* with verbs of feeling, *that*
tamquam, *just as if*

INTERROGATIVE WORDS AND PHRASES

Quam ob causam…? *For what reason …?*
Quantī…? *How much (in price)…?*
Quī…? Quae…? Quod…? interrog. adj., *What…? Which…?*
Quis…? Quid…? *Who…? What…?*

MISCELLANEOUS

Bonō animō es!/este! *Be of good mind! Cheer up!*
cāsū, *by chance, accidentally*
dē porcō datum est, *some pork was given*
Dī immortālēs! *Immortal gods! Good heavens!*
Euge! *Hurray!*
Quam…! *How…!*
quīdam, quaedam, quoddam, *a certain*
quā dē causā, *for this reason*
rēs urbānae, rērum urbānārum, f. pl., *affairs of the city/town*
summā celeritāte, *with the greatest speed, as fast as possible*

Activity VIIa

Translate into Latin:

1. A huge load of meat was being carried by slaves in the city during the day.

_____

_____

2. Nothing is carried by wagons in the city during the day.

_____

3. The pigs that had been fed by the butcher were being led to (his) shop by hand.

_____

_____

4. One of the pigs will be handed over to Pseudolus by the butcher for six denarii.

_____

_____

5. If Pseudolus gives/will have given eight denarii, that hare will be added to this pig by the butcher.

_____

_____

6. Pseudolus was delighted with this fat pig but not with that black one.

_____

_____

7. Aurelia will order Pseudolus to be punished.

_____

8. When the guests are/will have been courteously greeted by Cornelius in the atrium, they will be led into the dining room.

_____

_____

9. When the signal is/will have been given to the slaves, they will cut the pig and will carry the meat to the guests.

_____

_____

10. Cornelius was praised by his clients, although only scraps of chicken were given to them.

_____

_____

Activity VIIb
Supply the missing relative pronouns.

1. Orpheus, _____ Mūsae docuerant citharā lūdere, ad Plūtōnem dēscendit. (whom)

2. Orpheus, _____ uxor morte abrepta erat, dolōre oppressus est. (whose)

3. Orpheus appropinquāre cōnstituit Plūtōnī, ā _____ uxōrem petere volēbat. (whom)

4. Iānua Plūtōnis ā cane _____ ferōx erat et tria habēbat capita custōdiēbātur. (that)

5. Frusta cibī _____ Orpheus ad Cerberum coniēcit ā cane arrepta sunt. (that)

6. Orpheus uxōrem, _____ morte abrepta est, diū et dīligenter quaerēbat. (who)

7. Orpheus, _____ licet uxōrem suam redūcere, laetus est. (to whom)

8. Virō, _____ uxōrem suam ad lūcem redūcit, nōn licet ad eam respicere. (who)

9. Orpheus ad uxōrem, _____ dūcēbātur, diū nōn respexit. (who)

10. Eurydicē, ad _____ Orpheus tandem respexit, ad Plūtōnem retracta est neque ad lūcem umquam reddita est. (whom)

Activity VIIc

ACROSS
1. whose (sing.)
2. they were being guarded
5. carelessly
9. fire
10. to those men
12. and
13. you (pl.) will be overwhelmed
16. she is carried
18. they (masc.) have been invited
19. almost
21. scarcely
23. it
25. you (masc. sing.) have been seen
28. robbers (abl.)
30. of this one
31. beggar (dat. sing.)
35. she had been brought to or in
36. I will be carried

DOWN
1. dinner guests (nom.)
3. it had been thrown out
4. ever
6. them (abl.)
7. they are carried out
8. I eat
9. the same (neut.)
11. freedmen (abl.)
14. we will be cared for
15. lunch
17. we (masc.) had been sent
20. these (acc. masc.)
22. bedrooms
24. kitchen
26. his, her, its
27. to cook
29. to him, to her, to it
32. eggs
33. so
34. she

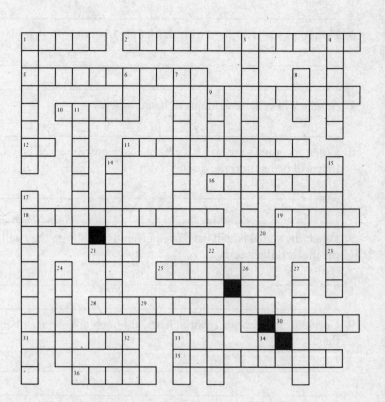

CHAPTER 34 THE COMMISSATIO

Activity 34a

Using the story at the beginning of Chapter 34 as a guide, answer the following questions in complete Latin sentences:

1. Quid convīvae induērunt? _____

_____

2. Quid Titus poposcit? _____

_____

3. Cūr Mesalla arbiter bibendī esse nōn dēbet? _____

_____

4. Cūr Gaius arbiter bibendī esse dēbet? _____

_____

5. Quō īnstrūmentō convīvae arbitrum bibendī rēctē creāre possunt? _____

_____

_____

6. Quōmodo Gaius omnia facere vult? _____

_____

7. Quid clāmāvērunt omnēs cum tālī ā Gaiō iactī sunt? _____

_____

8. Quōmodo Titus tālōs in fritillō pōnit? _____

_____

9. Quis Titō favet? _____

10. Quid facit Titus ubi arbiter bibendī creātus est? _____

_____

_____

_____

Activity 34b

Complete the Latin sentences to match the English cues:

1. Coquus cēnam _____ parāvit. (very good)

2. Convīvae _____ porcō dēlectābantur. (rather large)

3. Glīrēs erant _____ . (very fat)

4. Titus amīcō _____ in popīnā occurrerat. (rather bad)

5. Ea erat _____ omnium popīnārum in urbe. (worst)

6. Titus _____ _____ erat ubi in trīclīnium irrūpit. (very drunk)

7. "Numquam convīvam _____ vīdī," mussāvit Cornēlius. (worse)

(continued)

8. Titus _____ poculum arripuit et nimis vīnī bibit. (bigger)

9. Postquam poculum hausit, "Ego sum _____ omnium hominum!" clāmāvit. (luckiest)

10. "Tū es _____ et _____ omnium!" aliī mussāvērunt. (stupidest) (most annoying)

Activity 34c

Change the verbs in the following sentences from active to passive and make all other necessary changes. The first one is done for you.

1. Servī vīnum attulērunt.

   Vīnum ā servīs allātum est.

2. Servī omnibus convīvīs corōnās flōrum dederant.

   _____

   _____

3. Gaius apiō sē corōnāvit.

   _____

4. Titus multum vīnum in popīnā bibēbat.

   _____

5. Convīvae arbitrum bibendī tālīs creābunt.

   _____

   _____

6. Gaius aquam et vīnum prūdenter miscēbit.

   _____

   _____

7. Servī tālōs cum fritillō attulērunt et in mēnsā posuērunt.

   _____

   _____

8. Convīvae tālōs identidem mīsērunt.

   _____

9. Tandem Titus Venerem iēcit.

   _____

10. Titus maximum pōculum arripuit et hausit.

    _____

    _____

11. Ubi Titus secundum vīnī pōculum hauserit, servī eum vīnō oppressum auferent.

    _____

    _____

Activity 34d

Many English words are derived from the following Latin adjectives and their irregular comparative and superlative forms. Using an English dictionary as necessary, find and write definitions of each of the English words below:

1. **bonus, melior, optimus**

   a. bonanza _____

   b. bonbon _____

   c. bonus _____

   d. debonair _____

   e. ameliorate _____

   f. optimist _____

   g. optimum _____

2. **malus, peior, pessimus**

   a. malady _____

   b. malediction _____

   c. malice _____

   d. malign (verb) _____ (adjective) _____

   e. dismal _____

   f. pejorative _____

3. **magnus, maior, maximus**

   a. magnanimous _____

   b. magnate _____

   c. magnify _____

   d. majestic _____

   e. major (any one definition) _____

   f. majority _____

   g. maxim _____

   h. maximum _____

4. **parvus, minor, minimus**

   a. minimize _____

   b. minus _____

5. **multus (multī), plūs (plūrēs), plūrimus**

   a. multiple _____

   b. multiply _____

   c. multitude _____

   d. plural _____

   e. plurality _____

CHAPTER 35

CRIME

Activity 35a

In each of the following pairs of sentences, form a positive adverb from the adjective italicized in the first sentence and write the adverb in the blank in the second sentence. Then translate both sentences. The first one is done for you.

1. Eucleidēs *sēcūrus* est quod nihil timet. Eucleidēs per Subūram ___sēcūrē___ ambulat. ___Eucleides is unconcerned because he fears nothing. Eucleides walks___ ___unconcernedly through the Subura.___ _____

2. Cornēlius *sollicitus* est quod Eucleidēs nōndum rediit. Cornēlius hūc illūc _____ ambulat. _____

3. Flammae illīus incendiī *perīculōsae* sunt. Flammae ē fenestrīs _____ ēmittuntur. _____

4. Cornēlia *bonum* librum legit. Cornēlia _____ legere potest.

5. Eucleidēs vulnera *gravia* accēpit. Eucleidēs _____ vulnerātus est.

6. Syrus fābulam *brevem* puerīs nārrat. Syrus puerīs dē Pseudolō _____ nārrat.

7. Mulier *magnā* vōce exclāmat. Mulier flammīs _____ terrētur.

8. Cornēlius servōs *dīligentēs* habet. Servī omnia diē cēnae _____ parant.

9. Quam *fortis* est Eucleidēs! Eucleidēs baculō _____ sē dēfendit.

10. Viae sunt plēnae praedōnum *scelestōrum*. Praedōnēs viātōrēs miserōs _____ petunt. _____

Activity 35b

Fill in the blank in each of the following sentences with the form of the adverb indicated in parentheses. Then translate the sentence.

1. Eucleidēs _____ domum redierat. (**sērō**, superlative)

_____

2. Cornēlia ā miserīs līberīs _____ commovētur. (**magnopere**, superlative)

_____

_____

3. Eucleidēs apud frātrem _____ mānsit. (**diū**, superlative)

_____

4. Aurēlia speculum ancillae _____ adēmit. (**īrātē**, superlative)

_____

5. Titus _____ clientibus advēnit. (**sērō**, comparative)

_____

6. Gaius vīnum _____ quam Messalla miscēbit. (**prūdenter**, comparative)

_____

_____

7. Quamquam Eucleidēs quam _____ ambulābat, praedōnēs eum
   _____ cōnsecūtī sunt. (**celeriter**, superlative) (**facile**, superlative)

_____

_____

_____

8. Eucleidēs vīnum _____ bibit. (**lentē**, comparative)

_____

9. Titus _____ ēbrius Cornēliō fit. (**magnopere**, comparative)

_____

Activity 35c

Rewrite each of the following sentences, changing the comparison with *quam* to the ablative of comparison or vice versa, as in the examples below:

   Mārtiālis est prūdentior quam Eucleidēs.
                    or
   Mārtiālis est prūdentior Eucleide.

1. Titus est arbiter bibendī melior quam Messalla.

_____

2. Hoc aedificium est īnfirmius quam illud.

_____

3. Praedōnēs celerius Eucleide cucurrērunt.

_____

4. Eucleidēs sērius quam Titus advēnit.

_____

5. Cornēlia nihil miserius quam id spectāculum anteā vīderat.

_____

Activity 35d

Fill in the blanks with Latin words to match the English cues:

1. Eucleidēs noster _____ _____ accēpit. (a very serious wound)

2. Corpus Eucleidis fuit _____ _____ . (sprinkled with blood)

3. Eucleidēs _____ _____ diū mānserat. (at his brother's house)

4. Vulnera Eucleidis ā servīs _____ _____ _____ .
   (very carefully) (were bound up)

5. Titus vīnō _____ _____ subitō collāpsus est. (very greatly affected)

6. Eucleidēs ā _____ ab alterō praedōne _____ _____ . (the back) (was grabbed)

7. Eucleidēs amīcō _____ _____ vix poterat. (wise) (to believe)

8. Eucleidēs _____ _____ ad terram cecidit. (having been struck with a club)

9. Baculum quō Eucleidēs _____ sē dēfendēbat ā praedōnibus _____ correptum est. (very bravely) (easily)

10. Eucleidēs per Subūram _____ ambulābat. (too slowly)

11. Ubi Eucleidem vīdit, " _____ _____ !" exclāmāvit Cornēlius. (Good heavens!)

12. Praedōnēs omnem pecūniam _____ _____ . (from him) (they had taken away)

Activity 35e

Translate into Latin:

1. Eucleides finally arrived home very late.

   _____

2. He had been struck fiercely with a very big club.

   _____

3. His tunic was very dirty and sprinkled with blood.

   _____

4. Cornelius, however, was more worried than Eucleides.

   _____

5. "You have been rather seriously wounded," said Cornelius.

   _____

6. He ordered the wounds to be bound as quickly as possible.

   _____

7. The slaves were placing Eucleides on the couch.

   _____

8. Cornelius, greatly affected by this sight, said, "Move him more carefully!"

_____

_____

9. Cornelius then said to Eucleides very sadly, "You certainly have been most brave, Eucleides."

_____

_____

10. "When those robbers are found/will have been found, they will be punished most severely."

_____

Activity 35f

Complete each of the following sentences by choosing from the pool an English word of equivalent meaning to the word(s) in italics. (Consult an English dictionary for the meaning of the words in the pool.) In the space at the left, write the Latin word to which the English word chosen from the pool is related. The first one is done for you.

Latin Word	*If you have—*	*English Word*
1. sanguis	a *cheerful and confident* attitude in spite of misfortune, your attitude is	sanguine
2. _____	spread *false rumors* about people, you have cast…on them.	_____
3. _____	torn the *fibrous tissues* connecting your bones together, you have torn your	_____
4. _____	feelings that are *easily hurt*, you are	_____
5. _____	a *safe* place to keep valuables, that place is	_____
6. _____	fallen *face-down* on the ground, your position is	_____
7. _____	a *serious* illness, your illness is	_____
8. _____	made a *wise* decision, your decision was	_____
9. _____	reached the *top* of a mountain, you have reached its	_____
10. _____	a musical instrument played by *striking* it, you have a…instrument	_____

prone	sanguine	vulnerable	aspersions	secure
percussion	ligaments	grave	prudent	summit

CHAPTER 36

A LETTER

Activity 36a

Pretend you are Flavia and write in English a reply to Cornelia's letter. Include responses to what Cornelia says in each of the paragraphs of her letter. Write your letter on a separate sheet of paper.

Activity 36b

Give the dates for the following, first according to the English system and then according to the Roman system:

1. The first day of school this year _____

   _____

2. Halloween _____

   _____

3. Veterans Day _____

   _____

4. Thanksgiving _____

   _____

5. Saturnalia _____

   _____

6. Ground Hog Day _____

   _____

7. Valentine's Day _____

   _____

8. The first day of spring _____

   _____

9. Memorial Day _____

   _____

10. Independence Day _____

   _____

Activity 36c

You are frequently expected to deduce the meanings of certain Latin words that have not been given in the vocabulary. The most useful clue is usually the context of the story, but it is also possible to deduce the meanings of new words if you already know other words with the same root meaning. In the sets of words below, write the meaning of the word in boldface and then write definitions of the other words in the same line:

Noun	Verb	Adjective	Adverb
1. neglegentia	neglegere	neglegēns	**neglegenter**
_____	_____	_____	_____
2. timor	timēre	**timidus**	timidē
_____	_____	_____	_____

3. **ferōcitās**	(none)	ferōx	**ferōciter**
4. **difficultās**	(none)	difficilis	difficulter
5. **rēgnum**	rēgnāre	rēgālis	rēgāliter
6. **rēx** (rēgīna)	regere	rēgius	(none)
7. mors	morī	**mortuus**	(none)
8. īra	īrāscī	**īrātus**	īrātē
9. **nox**	pernoctāre	nocturnus	noctū

Activity 36d

S.D. (salūtem dīcit) is part of the standard greeting at the beginning of a Latin letter. Let us study the word *salūs, salūtis*, f.

1. **Look up this word in a Latin dictionary and find and list four different meanings for it:**

   _____   _____

   _____   _____

2. **Look further in the Latin dictionary and find another noun, a verb, an adjective, and an adverb formed from the same root as the word *salūs*. Write these under the heading Latin Words below:**

	Latin Words	*English Words*
Noun	_____	_____
Verb	_____	_____
Adjective	_____	_____
Adverb	_____	

3. **With the aid of an English dictionary if necessary, write the English words that have come from the Latin noun, verb, and adjective that you wrote above.**

CHAPTER 37

OFF TO SCHOOL

Activity 37a

In the space before each verb in the left-hand columns, write the letter of the verb in the right-hand columns that has the same or nearly the same meaning:

___ **1.** intrāverat	___ **8.** manēbam	**a.** proficīscētur		**h.** expertī sunt
___ **2.** dīxit	___ **9.** intrātis	**b.** loquēbāmur		**i.** locūtus est
___ **3.** discēdet	___ **10.** mānserāmus	**c.** profectus es		**j.** veritus sum
___ **4.** timent	___ **11.** dīcis	**d.** morābar		**k.** morātī erāmus
___ **5.** intrāvistis	___ **12.** timuī	**e.** loqueris		**l.** ingrediminī
___ **6.** discessistī	___ **13.** temptant	**f.** ingressus erat		**m.** ingressī estis
___ **7.** temptāvērunt	___ **14.** dīcēbāmus	**g.** verentur		**n.** experiuntur

Activity 37b

In the space(s) to the right of each sentence below, write the appropriate form of the verb(s) in parentheses to replace the italicized verb(s) in the sentence. The first one is done for you.

1. "Ego illō incendiō appropinquāre," inquit Cornēlia, "valdē *timuī*." (vereor)

   verita sum

2. Diū in urbe *manēbimus*. (moror) _____

3. In lūdō semper dīligenter labōrāre *vīs*. (cōnor) _____

4. Praedōnēs Eucleidem celerius *petīvērunt*. (cōnsequor) _____

5. "Nōlī, Sexte," inquit Palaemōn, "mē *vexāre*." (experior) _____

6. Convīvae multa inter sē *dīcēbant*. (loquor) _____

7. Eucleidēs vulnerātus in terram *ceciderat*. (collābor) _____

8. Mox laetissimī ē lūdō *exībitis*. (ēgredior) _____

9. "Herī," inquit Sextus, "ad lūdum invītus *iī*." (proficīscor) _____

10. Palaemōn Sextum crās *castīgābit*. (experior) _____

11. Cum Eucleidēs domum *redierit*, vulnera ā servīs ligābuntur. (regredior) _____

   _____

12. In illam caupōnam *intrāre nōlumus*. (ingredior) (vereor) _____

   _____

13. Quod iam Baiīs *discessistis*, vōs maximē dēsīderō. (proficīscor) _____

14. "Cavē, Tite," inquit Cornēlius. "In lectum *cadēs*." (collābor) _____

15. "*Age*, Sexte!" inquit Palaemōn. (ingredior) "Cūr extrā lūdum *manēs*?" (moror)

   _____ _____

Activity 37c

Fill in the blanks with Latin words to match the English cues (use deponent verbs wherever possible):

1. Cornēlia, quae in urbe _____ , ā Flāviā maximē _____ . (is staying) (is missed)

2. _____ puerīs necesse est ad lūdum _____ . (Every day) (to set out)

3. "Ille _____ fit _____ _____ peior," cōgitābat Sextus. (school) (day by day)

4. Puerī cum _____ _____ per viās ambulābant. (very learned tutor)

5. Eucleidēs rēs _____ _____ versūs Vergiliī docet. (more useful than)

6. Mulier, _____ Cornēlia in tertiō tabulātō cōnspexit, līberōs servāre _____ . (whom) (was trying)

7. "_____ laetē," inquit Euclcidēs, "ille _____ vōs accipiet!" (How...!) (secondary school teacher)

8. Coquus Cornēliī hanc cēnam _____ _____ parāvit. (as carefully as possible)

9. Eucleidēs _____ quam puerī semper _____ . (faster) (talks)

10. "Nisi statim in lūdum _____ , puerī," inquit grammaticus, "ā mē _____ ." (you enter/will have entered) (you will be reprimanded)

11. Praedōnēs Eucleidem domō frātris _____ facillimē _____ . (having left) (caught up to)

12. Sextus haec cōgitābat: "Lūdum nōn amō _____ ille grammaticus mē nōn amat." (or)

13. _____ puerīs ab Eucleide _____ . (A lantern) (was being carried in front)

14. Ubi puerī _____ sūmpsērunt, "Agite," inquit Eucleidēs, " _____ mē!" (breakfast) (follow!)

15. "_____ _____ illōs Vergiliī versūs, puerī?" rogat grammaticus. (Do you remember)

Activity 37d

Translate into Latin, using deponent verbs wherever possible:

1. Having set out before light, the boys were unwillingly following Eucleides to school.

_____

_____

2. Soon, however, they ran ahead, and Eucleides was trying very hard to catch up to them.

_____

_____

3. Palacmon, that most learned teacher, was waiting at the door of the school.

_____

_____ (continued)

4. The boys were not afraid to go into the school because Palaemon greeted them very courteously.

_____

_____

5. Having entered the school, Marcus said to Sextus, "How courteously this teacher receives us!"

_____

_____

6. Sextus replied to him, "Wait for a short time, Marcus. He has not tested us yet."

_____

_____

Activity 37e

Next to each English word in the pool below, write the Latin word to which it is related; then write each English word in the blank in the appropriate sentence below:

moratorium	_____	regressive	_____
sequel	_____	loquacious	_____
consequence	_____	eloquent	_____
erudite	_____	colloquial	_____
utility	_____	pedagogical	_____

1. Eucleides was so _____ , the boys found it difficult to get a word in edgewise.

2. Although he was twelve years old, the boy's _____ behavior often made him appear to be much younger.

3. Because of a riot, a _____ of ten years was imposed on gladiatorial contests in Pompeii.

4. _____ is more important than appearance; it does not matter how good something looks if it is of no use.

5. The senator delivered a most _____ speech; everyone was deeply moved by the power of his words.

6. Eucleides did not approve of the _____ language of the streets, and he forbade the boys to use such slang.

7. Eucleides preferred the _____ language of scholars to the speech of the common people.

8. The *Odyssey* is a _____ to the *Iliad*, since the events of the story of Odysseus follow the destruction of Troy.

9. "Palaemon does not use sound _____ technique," complained Sextus. "I never learn anything!"

10. As a _____ of his lack of proper study, Sextus was unable to respond correctly when called upon in school.

This list includes positive, comparative, and superlative adjectives from Chapter 34 and adverbs in the three degrees from Chapter 35.

NOUNS

1st Declension

arānea, -ae, f., *cobweb*

corōna, -ae, f., *garland, crown*

cūra, -ae, f., *care*

hedera, -ae, f., *ivy*

Kalendae, -ārum, f. pl., *the Kalends (1st day in the month)*

lanterna, -ae, f., *lantern*

Nōnae, -ārum, f. pl., *Nones*

rosa, -ae, f., *rose*

scriblīta, -ae, f., *tart or pastry with cheese filling*

Subūra, -ae, f., *Subura (a section of Rome off the Forum, known for its night life)*

2nd Declension

apium, -ī, n., *parsley*

arbiter, arbitrī, m., *master*

   arbiter bibendī, *master of the drinking*

Brundisium, -ī, n., *Brundisium*

   Brundisiī, *at Brundisium*

   Brundisium, *to Brundisium*

   Brundisiō, *from Brundisium*

convīvium, -ī, n., *feast, banquet*

cyathus, ī, m., *small ladle, measure (of wine)*

deus, -ī, m., *god*

fritillus, -ī, m., *cylindrical box*

grammaticus, -ī, m., *secondary school teacher*

iēntāculum, -ī, n., *breakfast*

lūdus, -ī, m., *game, school*

magister, magistrī, m. *schoolmaster, master, captain*

merum, -ī, n., *undiluted wine*

modus, -ī, m., *way, method*

paedagōgus, -ī, m., *tutor*

paulum, -ī, n., *a small amount, a little*

pīstrīnum, -ī, n., *bakery*

sacculus, -ī, m., *small bag used for holding money*

tālī, -ōrum, m. pl., *knucklebones*

tergum, -ī, n., *back, rear*

unguentum, -ī, n., *ointment, perfume*

Vergilius, -ī, m., *Vergil (Roman poet)*

3rd Declension

adulēscēns, adulēscentis, m., *young man, youth*

amor, amōris, m., *love*

canis, canis, m./f., *dog, the lowest throw of the knucklebones*

collis, collis, gen. pl., **collium**, m., *hill*

commissātiō, commissātiōnis, f., *drinking party*

cōnsul, cōnsulis, m., *consul*

Cupīdō, Cupīdinis, m., *Cupid (the son of Venus)*

difficultās, difficultātis, f., *difficulty*

flōs, flōris, m., *flower*

fūstis, fūstis, gen. pl., **fūstium**, m., *club, cudgel*

Herculēs, Herculis, m., *Hercules (Greek hero)*

sal, salis, m., *salt, wit*

salūs, salūtis, f., *greetings*

sēniō, sēniōnis, m., *the six (in throwing knucklebones)*

timor, timōris, m., *fear*

Venus, Veneris, f., *Venus; the highest throw of the knucklebones*

vulnus, vulneris, n., *wound*

4th Declension

Īdūs, Īduum, f. pl., *the Ides*

Indeclinable

nīl, *nothing*

ADJECTIVES

1st and 2nd Declension

affectus, -a, -um, *affected, overcome*

candidus, -a, -um, *white, fair-skinned, beautiful*

certus, -a, -um, *certain*

ēbrius, -a, -um, *drunk*

ērudītus, -a, -um, *learned, scholarly*

foedus, -a, -um, *filthy, disgusting*

lentus, -a, -um, *slow*

merus, -a, -um, *pure*

paucī, -ae, -a, *few*

prōnus, -a, -um, *face down*

rēctus, -a, -um, *right, proper*

sēcūrus, -a, -um, *carefree, unconcerned*

sextus, -a, -um, *sixth*

summus, -a, -um, *greatest, very great, the top of…*

venustus, -a, -um, *charming*

Months

Iānuārius, -a, -um, *January*

Februārius, -a, -um, *February*

Mārtius, -a, -um, *March*

Aprīlis, -is, -e, *April*

Maius, -a, -um, *May*

Iūnius, -a, -um, *June*

Iūlius, -a, -um, *July*

Augustus, -a, -um, *August*

September, Septembris, Septembre, *September*

Octōber, Octōbris, Octōbre, *October*

November, Novembris, Novembre, *November*

December, Decembris, Decembre, *December*

1st and 2nd Declension Adjectives: Positive, Comparative, and Superlative

miser, misera, miserum, *unhappy, miserable, wretched*

   miserior, miserior, miserius, gen., **miseriōris**, *more/rather wretched*

   miserrimus, -a, -um, *most/very wretched*

molestus, -a, -um, *troublesome, annoying*

molestior, molestior, molestius, gen., **molestiōris**, *more/rather annoying*

molestissimus, -a, -um, *most/very annoying*

pulcher, pulchra, pulchrum, *beautiful, pretty, handsome*

pulchrior, pulchrior, pulchrius, gen., **pulchriōris**, *more/rather beautiful/pretty/handsome*

pulcherrimus, -a, -um, *most/very beautiful/pretty/handsome*

1st and 2nd Declension with Irregular Comparatives and Superlatives

bonus, -a, -um, *good*

melior, melior, melius, gen., **meliōris**, *better*

optimus, -a, -um, *best, very good, excellent*

magnus, -a, -um, *big, great, large, loud (voice, laugh)*

maior, maior, maius, gen., **maiōris**, *bigger, greater*

maximus, -a, -um, *biggest, greatest, very great, very large*

malus, -a, -um, *bad, evil*

peior, peior, peius, gen., **peiōris**, *worse*

pessimus, -a, -um, *worst*

multī, -ae, -a, *many*

plūrēs, plūrēs, plūra, gen., **plūrium**, *more*

plūrimī, -ae, -a, *most, very many*

multus, -a, -um, *much*

plūs, plūris, *more*

plūrimus, -a, -um, *most, very much*

parvus, -a, -um, *small*

minor, minor, minus, gen., **minōris**, *smaller*

minimus, -a, -um, *very small, smallest*

3rd Declension

abstinēns, abstinentis + abl., *refraining from*

audāx, audācis, *bold*

difficilis, -is, -e, *difficult*

dīligēns, dīligentis, *diligent, painstaking, thorough*

dissimilis, -is, -e, *dissimilar*

ferōx, ferōcis, *fierce*

gracilis, -is, -e, *slender*

gravis, -is, -e, *heavy, serious*

humilis, -is, -e, *humble*

Quirīnālis, -is, -e, *Quirinal (Hill)*

similis, -is, -e, *similar*

suāvis, -is, -e, *sweet, delightful*

trīstis, -is, -e, *sad*

ūtilis, -is, -e, *useful*

vehemēns, vehementis, *violent*

vetus, veteris, *old*

3rd Declension Positive, Comparative, and Superlative

ācer, ācris, ācre, *keen*

ācrior, ācrior, ācrius, gen., **ācriōris**, *keener, rather keen*

ācerrimus, -a, -um, *keenest, very keen*

brevis, -is, -e, *short*

brevior, brevior, brevius, gen., **breviōris**, *shorter, rather short*

brevissimus, -a, -um, *shortest, very short*

celer, celeris, celere, *swift*

celerior, celerior, celerius, gen., **celeriōris**, *swifter, rather swift*

celerrimus, -a, -um, *swiftest, very swift*

facilis, -is, -e, *easy*

facilior, facilior, facilius, gen., **faciliōris**, *easier, rather easy*

facillimus, -a, -um, *easiest, very easy*

fēlīx, fēlīcis, *lucky*

fēlīcior, fēlīcior, fēlīcius, gen., **fēlīciōris**, *luckier, rather lucky*

fēlīcissimus, -a, -um, *luckiest, very lucky*

fidēlis, -is, -e, *faithful*

fidēlior, fidēlior, fidēlius, gen., **fidēliōris**, *more faithful, rather faithful*

fidēlissimus, -a, -um, *most faithful, very faithful*

prūdēns, prūdentis, *wise*

prūdentior, prūdentior, prūdentius, gen., **prūdentiōris**, *wiser, rather wise*

prūdentissimus, -a, -um, *wisest, very wise*

Indeclinable

vīgintī, *twenty*

VERBS

1st Conjugation

castīgō, -āre, -āvī, -ātus, *to rebuke, reprimand*

corōnō, -āre, -āvī, -ātus, *to crown*

creō, -āre, -āvī, -ātus, *to appoint*

dōnō, -āre, -āvī, -ātus, *to give*

invocō, -āre, -āvī, -ātus, *to invoke, call upon*

ligō, -āre, -āvī, -ātus, *to bind up*

2nd Conjugation

misceō, miscēre, miscuī, mixtus, *to mix*

persuādeō, persuādēre, persuāsī, persuāsus, *to make something (acc.) agreeable to someone (dat.); to persuade someone of something*

placeō, -ēre, -uī + dat., *to please*

3rd Conjugation

adimō, adimere, adēmī, adēmptus + dat., *to take away (from)*

concurrō, concurrere, concurrī, concursūrus, *to run together, rush up*

condō, condere, condidī, conditus, *to found, establish*

crēdō, crēdere, crēdidī, crēditus + dat., *to trust, believe*

dēfendō, dēfendere, dēfendī, dēfēnsus, *to defend*

poscō, poscere, poposcī, *to demand, ask for*

sinō, sinere, sīvī, situs, *to allow*

3rd Conjugation -*iō*

corripiō, corripere, corripuī, correptus, *to seize, grab*

percutiō, percutere, percussī, percussus, *to strike*

4th Conjugation
hauriō, haurīre, hausī, haustus, *to drain*

Irregular
fīō, fierī, factus sum, *to become, be made, be done, happen*

praeferō, praeferre, praetulī, praelātus, *to carry X* (acc.) *in front of Y* (dat.)

Deponent Verbs

1st Conjugation
cōnor, cōnārī, cōnātus sum, *to try*

moror, morārī, morātus sum, *to delay, remain, stay*

2nd Conjugation
vereor, verērī, veritus sum, *to be afraid, fear*

3rd Conjugation
collābor, collābī, collāpsus sum, *to collapse*

colloquor, colloquī, collocūtus sum, *to converse, speak together*

cōnsequor, cōnsequī, cōnsecūtus sum, *to catch up to, overtake*

loquor, loquī, locūtus sum, *to speak, talk*

proficīscor, proficīscī, profectus sum, *to set out, leave*

sequor, sequī, secūtus sum, *to follow*

3rd Conjugation *-iō*
ēgredior, ēgredī, ēgressus sum, *to go out, leave*

ingredior, ingredī, ingressus sum, *to go in, enter*

regredior, regredī, regressus sum, *to go back, return*

4th Conjugation
experior, experīrī, expertus sum, *to test, try*

PREPOSITION
ante + acc., *before, in front of*

ADVERBS
bene, *well*
  melius, *better*
  optimē, *best, very well, excellently*
breviter, *briefly*
  brevius, *more/rather briefly*
  brevissimē, *most/very briefly*
celeriter, *quickly*
  celerius, *more/rather quickly*
  celerrimē, *most/very quickly*
certē, *certainly*
  certius, *more/rather certainly*
contrā, *in return*
cotīdiē, *daily, every day*
diū, *for a long time*
  diūtius, *longer*
  diūtissimē, *longest*
facile, *easily*
  facilius, *more/rather easily*
  facillimē, *most/very easily*
fēlīciter, *well, happily, luckily*
  fēlīcius, *more/rather happily*
  fēlīcissimē, *most/very happily*
fortiter, *bravely*
  fortius, *more/rather bravely*
  fortissimē, *most/very bravely*
hūc, *here, to here*
laetē, *happily*
  laetius, *more/rather happily*
  laetissimē, *most/very happily*
libenter, *gladly*
  libentius, *more/rather gladly*
  libentissimē, *most/very gladly*
longē, *far*
magnopere, *greatly*
  magis, *more*
  maximē, *most, very much, very*
male, *badly*
  peius, *worse*
  pessimē, *worst*
multum, *much*
  plūs, *more*
  plūrimum, *most*
nimis, *too much*

paulātim, *gradually, little by little*
paulum, *little*
  minus, *less*
  minimē, *least*
prīdiē, adv. + acc., *on the day before*
prūdenter, *wisely, sensibly*
  prūdentius, *more/rather sensibly*
  prūdentissimē, *most/very sensibly*
quam, *than*
quam + superlative adj. or adv., *as…as possible*
  quam celerrimē, *as quickly as possible*
Quam…! *How…! What a…!*
Quam…? *How…?*
rēctē, *rightly, properly*
  rēctius, *more/rather properly*
  rēctissimē, *most/very properly*
rūrsus, *again*
saepe, *often*
  saepius, *more often*
  saepissimē, *most/very often*
sānē, *certainly, of course*
sērō, *late*
  sērius, *later*
  sērissimē, *latest*
strēnuē, *strenuously, hard*

CONJUNCTIONS
etiamsī, *even if*
-que, *and*
seu = sīve, *or if*
-ve, enclitic conj., *or*
vel, *or*

MISCELLANEOUS
ad tempus, *on time*
in diēs, *every day, day by day*
memoriā tenēre, *to remember*
nē…quidem, *not even*
plūs vīnī, *more wine*
quō…eō…, *the (more)…the (more)…*
S.D. = salūtem dīcere, *to send greetings*
S.P.D. = salūtem plūrimam dīcere, *to send fondest greetings*
sīs = sī vīs, *if you wish, please*

Activity VIIIa

Translate into Latin, using deponent verbs wherever possible:

1. No one is a wiser master of the drinking than Gaius.

   _____

2. He mixes the wine and water more sensibly than all the others.

   _____

3. Titus, who drank too much wine, suddenly collapsed and (use a perfect participle and do not translate "and") was carried out of the dining room as quickly as possible.

   _____

4. When two men who were carrying clubs rushed from a cookshop, Eucleides tried to walk faster.

   _____

   _____

5. Overcome with fear, Eucleides returned home in as short a time as possible.

   _____

   _____

6. Valerius will arrive home from Brundisium in a few days.

   _____

7. How happy Cornelia will be to see him! (= How gladly Cornelia will see him!)

   _____

8. She will be even happier to see Flavia.

   _____

9. Marcus and Sextus must (use **necesse est** + dat. + infin.) set out for school before dawn.

   _____

10. Sextus, however, wants to stay home because he cannot remember Vergil's verses.

    _____

11. Palaemon, the rather learned school teacher, will try to teach the boys very many useful things.

    _____

    _____

Activity VIIIb

Find and circle the Latin words for the English clues listed below. Words may go in a horizontal, vertical, or diagonal direction, but they do not go backward.

1. I am delaying
2. care
3. to call upon
4. he drained
5. the best (neut.)
6. more
7. as quickly as possible
8. smallest (neut.)
9. gradually
10. luckier (gen. sing.)

11. most learned (fem. acc. pl.)
12. August
13. easiest (masc.)
14. with a club
15. they followed (dep.)
16. sweet
17. he tried (dep.)
18. worst (neut.)
19. more bravely
20. he has returned (dep.)

21. greater (fem.)
22. rather foolish (masc. acc. pl.)
23. he is talking (dep.)
24. useful
25. filthy
26. most beautiful (fem.)
27. hill
28. they went out (dep.)
29. I am afraid (dep.)
30. very sensibly

```
P  R  U  D  E  N  T  I  S  S  I  M  E  C  O  L  L  I  S  Q
A  T  H  A  N  P  K  N  T  R  A  J  A  N  F  U  S  T  E  U
U  C  A  E  C  U  D  V  A  U  G  U  S  T  U  S  T  E  C  A
L  O  U  G  F  L  G  O  P  T  I  M  U  M  H  I  U  I  U  M
A  N  S  R  K  C  L  C  J  U  N  O  M  P  A  N  L  O  T  C
T  A  I  E  A  H  Q  A  R  U  C  S  W  A  B  G  T  X  I  E
I  T  T  S  T  E  U  R  C  F  O  E  D  U  S  D  I  E  S  L
M  U  V  S  F  R  G  E  H  O  N  I  V  I  A  M  O  S  U  E
A  S  N  I  O  R  F  P  Q  R  S  R  E  S  V  A  R  T  N  R
U  E  W  S  X  I  E  A  U  T  I  B  R  C  L  M  E  D  T  R
F  S  N  U  O  M  L  P  E  I  L  R  E  S  A  E  S  T  F  I
V  T  C  N  G  A  I  Q  H  U  I  W  O  M  I  N  I  M  U  M
D  A  F  T  I  L  C  M  U  S  U  N  R  O  S  W  X  T  P  E
E  R  U  D  I  T  I  S  S  I  M  A  S  A  U  T  I  L  I  S
R  S  G  F  E  R  O  D  I  C  C  E  X  I  M  O  X  S  U  E
B  U  C  T  M  O  R  O  R  A  A  D  U  B  A  E  V  A  F  U
F  A  C  I  L  L  I  M  U  S  P  E  S  S  I  M  U  M  S  V
H  V  Q  U  I  G  S  P  H  A  E  I  W  C  O  L  X  D  H  M
N  I  O  L  O  Q  U  I  T  U  R  Q  U  A  R  F  I  G  L  E
I  S  B  A  U  X  R  E  G  R  E  S  S  U  S  E  S  T  J  R
```

THE LESSONS BEGIN

Activity 38a

Using the story at the beginning of Chapter 38 as a guide, answer the following questions in complete Latin sentences:

1. Quot mēnsēs abhinc puerī prīmum librum Aenēidis lēgērunt? _____

_____

2. Quot annōs Graecī Troiam obsidēbant? _____

_____

3. Quid urbs capta passa est? _____

4. Quī ūnā cum Aenēā ē Troiā captā effūgērunt? _____

_____

5. Cūr effūgērunt? _____

_____

6. Quid passī sunt Troiānī ubi ē Siciliā profectī sunt? _____

_____

7. Quō Aenēās āctus est? _____

8. Cuius ad urbem Aenēās advēnit? _____

_____

9. Quōmodo Dīdō Aenēān accēpit? _____

10. Quid Aenēās in convīviō fēcit? _____

_____

11. Quid fēcērunt omnēs convīvae? _____

12. Ubi Aenēās sēdit? _____

13. Quālem dolōrem Aenēās renovat? _____

_____

Activity 38b

Complete the following sentences, which list the kings of Rome in chronological order:

1. Rōmulus erat prīmus rēx Rōmānōrum.

2. Numa Pompilius erat _____ rēx Rōmānōrum.

3. Tullus Hostīlius erat _____ rēx Rōmānōrum.

4. Ancus Marcius erat _____ rēx Rōmānōrum.

5. Tarquinius Prīscus erat _____ rēx Rōmānōrum.

6. Servius Tullius erat _____ rēx Rōmānōrum.

7. Tarquinius Superbus erat _____ rēx Rōmānōrum.

rēx, rēgis, m., *king*

Activity 38c

Complete the following list of the months of the year:

1. Aprīlis est quārtus mēnsis annī.

2. September est _____ mēnsis annī.

3. Maius est _____ mēnsis annī.

4. November est _____ mēnsis annī.

5. Iūnius est _____ mēnsis annī.

6. Februārius est _____ mēnsis annī.

7. Iūlius est _____ mēnsis annī.

8. Mārtius est _____ mēnsis annī.

9. Octōber est _____ mēnsis annī.

10. Augustus est _____ mēnsis annī.

11. Iānuārius est _____ mēnsis annī.

12. December est _____ mēnsis annī.

Activity 38d

Look up "Calendar" in an encyclopedia or other reference work, and find answers to the following questions:

1. When did January rather than March become the first month of the year?
_____

2. The month named **Iūlius** was originally named **Quīntīlis**. Why did it have this name?
_____

3. In whose honor was the month **Quīntīlis** renamed **Iūlius**? When was it renamed?
_____

4. What had this man done to deserve this honor? _____
_____

5. When did he do it? _____

6. The month named **Augustus** was originally named **Sextīlis**. Why? _____
_____

7. In whose honor was this month given the name **Augustus**? _____
_____

Activity 38e

At the left is a complete list of the cardinal numbers in Latin from one to twenty, in numerical order. Using your knowledge of the Latin numbers, deduce the meaning of each of the Italian and French numbers (in scrambled order) at the right and write the corresponding Arabic numbers (1, 2, 3, etc.) on the lines provided:

Latin	Italian		French		Latin	Italian		French	
ūnus, -a, -um	quattro	___	deux	___	tredecim *or*				
duo, -ae, -o	dodici	___	dix	___	decem (et) trēs	diciannove	___	dix-neuf	___
trēs, trēs, tria	sei	___	quatre	___	quattuordecim	sette	___	quinze	___
quattuor	uno	___	six	___	quīndecim	due	___	seize	___
quīnque	sedici	___	dix-sept	___	sēdecim	quattordici	___	treize	___
sex	nove	___	onze	___	septendecim	venti	___	huit	___
septem	diciassette	___	quatorze	___	duodēvīgintī *or*				
octō	dieci	___	sept	___	octōdecim	diciotto	___	un	___
novem	cinque	___	cinq	___	undēvīgintī *or*				
decem	quindici	___	douze	___	novendecim	undici	___	dix-huit	___
ūndecim	tre	___	neuf	___	vīgintī	tredici	___	trois	___
duodecim	otto	___	vingt	___					

CHAPTER 39 — A LESSON FOR SEXTUS

Activity 39a

Read each of the following sentences and write the translation of the italicized words only:

1. Cornēliī vīllam rūsticam *Baiīs* habent. _____

2. Aestāte *Baiās* iter facere solent. _____

3. Cornēliī ante fīnem aestātis *Baiīs* profecti *domum* rediērunt.

   _____   _____

4. Eucleidēs līberōs *domī* cūrāre solet. _____

5. Eucleidēs puerōs cotīdiē *domō* ēdūcit quod *Rōmae* necesse est eīs ad lūdum īre.

   _____   _____

6. Līberōs, dum *in urbe Rōmā* habitant, haec dē Aenēā docēbit grammaticus.

   _____

7. Aenēās *Troiae* multōs annōs habitābat. _____

8. Aenēās *Troiā* cum comitibus iter fēcit. _____

9. Aenēās *Troiam* numquam rediit. _____

10. Aenēās *Dēlum* nāvigāvit. _____

11. Aenēās *Dēlī* breve modo tempus morātus est. _____

12. Aenēās *Dēlō* brevī tempore profectus est. _____

13. Aenēās *ā Siciliā* profectus *ad Āfricam* tempestāte āctus est.

   _____

14. Aenēās *Carthāginem* sextā hōrā pervēnit. _____

15. Aenēās ā Dīdōne pulchrā *Carthāginī* acceptus est. _____

16. Aenēae tamen *Carthāgine* prīmā lūce nāvigāre necesse est.

   _____

17. Aenēās *ab Āfricā* profectus *ad Italiam* nāvigāvit.

   _____

18. Aenēās Troiam novam *in Italiā* condere volēbat. _____

Activity 39b

Circle the appropriate Latin word or phrase for the italicized English expression in each sentence below:

1. Cornēliī Rōmae *for many years* habitābant.

   multīs annīs   multōs annōs   multī annī

2. Abhinc *three months* ē Bīthȳniā ēgressus sum.

   tribus mēnsibus   trēs mēnsēs   trium mēnsum

3. Cornēliī *in a few months* ad vīllam rūsticam redībunt.

   paucōs mēnsēs   paucī mēnsēs   paucīs mēnsibus

4. Illī canēs *for the whole night* in viīs lātrābant.

   tōtam noctem   tōtā nocte   tōtīs noctibus

5. Prīnceps lūdōs circēnsēs *for four days* fēcit.

   quārtō diē   quattuor diēbus   quattuor diēs

6. Cornēlius ad Forum *at the second hour* profectus est.

   secundam hōram   secundā hōrā   duās hōrās

7. Nāvēs Aenēae *for many days* hūc illūc āctae sunt.

   multōs diēs   multīs diēbus   multī diēs

8. Vergilius, poēta praeclārus, *in his 50th year* mortuus est.

   quīnquāgintā annōs   quīnquāgēsimō annō   quīnquāgēsimum annum

9. Aenēās ab Asiā *a few years before* vēnerat.

   paucōs annōs antequam   paucīs annīs   paucīs ante annīs

10. Aenēās *in three years* ad Italiam nāvigābit.

    trēs annī   tribus annīs   trēs annōs

11. Vergilius, *when he was eight years old*, Cremōnam missus est.

    octō annōs nātus   octō annīs   octō annīs nātus

12. *At that time* urbs Troia ā Graecīs obsidēbātur.

    ea tempora   eō tempore   id tempus

Activity 39c

Rewrite each of the following sentences, replacing the italicized phrase with the appropriate form of the noun in parentheses. Include or delete the preposition, as is appropriate. The first one is done for you.

1. Cornēliī *ab vīllā* discēdere parant. (**Baiae, Baiārum,** f. pl.)

    Cornēliī Baiīs discēdere parant.

2. Cornēlia *ad vīllam* redīre vult. (**Baiae**)

    _____

3. Flāvia *in oppidō* habitābat. (**Baiae**)

    _____

4. Cornēlius *ad urbem* revocātus erat. (**Rōma, -ae,** f.)

    _____

5. Cornēlius, dum *in Cūriā* morātur, ā prīncipe cōnsultus est. (**Rōma**)

    _____

6. Aenēās cum Dīdōne *in Āfricā* morārī volēbat. (**Carthāgō, Carthāginis,** f.)

    _____

7. Comitēs Aenēae *ab Āfricā* nāvigāre volēbant. (**Carthāgō**)

    _____

8. Hannibal cum patre *ad Hispāniam* iit. (**Gādēs, Gādium,** f. pl.)

    _____

9. Hannibal *ex Hispāniā* cum mīlitibus discessit. (**Gādēs**)

    _____

10. Hannibal *in Āfricā* nōn relictus erat. (**domus**)

    _____

Activity 39d

Fill in the blanks with Latin words to match the English cues:

1. Cornēlius _____ merīdiem domō exiit. (before)

2. Vergilius, _____ Brundisium pervēnit, diūtissimē _____ . (before) (had been ill)

3. Grammaticus, quī _____ sūmpsit, Sextum _____ invenīre potest. (the cane) (nowhere)

4. Pater _____ dōnum tibi _____ mihi dedit. (the same...as)

5. Cornēliī aestāte ad vīllam rūsticam _____ . (will move their home)

6. Aenēās _____ _____ locūtus est. (to his companions) (in this way)

7. Nisi vōs omnēs statim _____ , Palaemōn erit _____ . (you become/will become silent) (very angry)

8. Omnēs discipulī _____ _____ Sextum obdormientem cōnspexērunt. (except Marcus)

9. Sextus ā grammaticō _____ vigilāre cōnābātur. (warned)

10. Sextus ē somnō _____ , "Ō mē miserum," inquit, "ego _____ sum."
    (having awakened) (very sick)

11. Aenēās cum _____ nāvibus ad Āfricam nāvigāvit. (few)

12. Sextus _____ Vergiliī _____ nōn vult. (verses) (to study)

13. Cremōna et Mantua sunt _____ Italiae _____ . (towns) (northern)

14. Corpus Vergiliī Neāpolī _____ _____ . (was buried)

15. Aulus multa dē fābulā _____ . (omitted)

Activity 39e
Translate into Latin:

1. After one student finished reciting, another spoke in this way.

   _____

   _____

2. "Aeneas, having set out from Troy, was wandering for many years: to Thrace, then
   Delos, then Crete, and finally to Sicily."

   _____

   _____

3. "He delayed nowhere but kept looking for Hesperia, which is the same land as Italy."

   _____

   _____

4. "A very great storm drove Aeneas (**Aenēān**) to Carthage."

   _____

5. "Carthage had been founded by Dido in Africa."

   _____

6. "Aeneas, captured by love, was delaying there for many days."

   _____

7. "He did not notice his very unhappy companions."

   _____

8. "In the middle of the night, however, Aeneas was warned by the gods and set out toward
   Italy at first light."

   _____

   _____

Activity 39f

For each of the following Latin words, give the related Latin verb and its meaning:

	Related Latin Verb	*Meaning*
1. recitātiō, recitātiōnis, f., a reading aloud	_____	_____
2. nāvigātiō, nāvigātiōnis, f., a sailing	_____	_____
3. migrātiō, migrātiōnis, f., a moving of one's home	_____	_____
4. monitor, monitōris, m., a prompter	_____	_____
5. mōnstrum, -ī, n., a supernatural event, portent	_____	_____
6. mors, mortis, f., death	_____	_____
7. sepulcrum, -ī, n., tomb	_____	_____

Activity 39g

Fill in the blanks in the following sentences with English words derived from the Latin words in Activity 39f:

1. The body was placed in the _____ .

2. The shallow depth of the river made _____ difficult.

3. The boys' progress at school was _____ carefully by Eucleides.

4. The students listened carefully as Palaemon delivered a _____ of verses from the *Aeneid*.

5. Eucleides' wounds were not serious enough to be _____ , and so he recovered.

6. The _____ of people from the countryside into the city created problems of overpopulation.

7. Hercules had to defeat the Hydra, a snakelike _____ with several heads.

Activity 40a

Complete the following sentences with participles, keeping to the English cues.
Make the participles agree in gender, case, and number with the italicized words.

1. *Pater* Sextī in Asiam _____ Sextum in Italiā relīquit. (setting out)

2. *Sextus* Baiīs _____ ad lītus saepe ībat. (living)

3. *Sextus* magnā vōce _____ *Dāvum* in hortō _____ saepe vexābat. (shouting) (working)

4. Lupus *puerīs* in silvā _____ appropinquāvit. (walking)

5. Vōx *Marcī* lupum _____ ā Cornēliā audīta est. (driving away)

6. Deinde Cornēlia *Marcum* magnō rāmō lupum _____ vīdit. (driving away)

7. Sextus nūllum auxilium *Marcō* lupum _____ tulit. (driving away)

8. *Sextus* lupum _____ arborem ascendit. (fearing)

9. *Cornēliīs* iter Rōmam _____ magnum malum accidit. (making)

10. Sextus *russātīs* semper _____ favet. (winning)

11. Palaemōn *Sextum* semper discere _____ saepe verberat. (desiring)

12. Sextus *Palaemonī* difficillima _____ respondēre nōn poterat. (asking)

13. Cēterī *puerī* dē Hesperiā _____ rēctē respondēre potuērunt. (knowing)

14. *Aenēās* ipse _____ ubi esset Hesperia ad Āfricam errāvit. (not knowing)

15. Magister *Sextum* dē Hesperiā _____ crūdēlissimē verberāvit. (not knowing)

16. *Sextus* domum _____ ā Cornēliō arcessītus est. (entering)

17. Cornēlius *Sextum* rem explicāre _____ iterum pūnīvit. (trying)

18. *Sextus* miser et valdē _____ epistulam ad patrem mittit. (being sick)

Activity 40b

Translate the following sentences into Latin:

1. At Baiae Sextus used to watch the boats approaching the shore.

   _____

   _____

2. Once Marcus was in a tree and from there he caught sight of two wolves attacking the girls.

   _____

   _____

3. Marcus did not dare to leap down.

   _____

   _____

4. Sextus, learning nothing in school, was often beaten on account of the bad temper of the teacher, Palaemon.

_____

_____

5. Palaemon was always in the habit of asking Sextus very difficult things.

_____

_____

6. Today Sextus did not rejoice when Palaemon asked him about Hesperia.

_____

_____

7. Since Sextus did not know where Hesperia was, Palaemon beat him with his stick.

_____

_____

8. As soon as Sextus arrived home, he was punished again.

_____

_____

9. Cornelius did not even let him speak.

_____

_____

10. "Father, return home as soon as possible!" Sextus begged in a letter.

_____

_____

Activity 40c
Using an English dictionary, find and write the meanings of the following words, which are derived from words in the vocabulary for Chapter 40:

1. cupidity _____

2. audacious _____

3. desultory _____

4. valediction _____

5. repellent   a. _____

              b. _____

6. valid _____

7. invalid (noun) _____

        (adjective) _____

8. ignoramus _____

9. littoral _____

Activity 41a

Rewrite each of the following sentences by (1) dropping the relative pronoun (in boldface) and (2) replacing the verb (also in boldface) with a present participle. Make the participle agree in gender, case, and number with the italicized word. Then translate the new sentence. The first one is done for you.

1. *Cornēlia*, **quae** sōla **sedet**, tēlam texēbat. _Cornēlia sōla sedēns tēlam texēbat. Sitting_

   alone, Cornelia was weaving fabric. _____

   _____

2. Cornēlia *mātrem*, **quae ingreditur**, subitō cōnspexit. _____

   _____

   _____

3. *Cornēliae* miserae, **quae** domī **manet**, urbs Rōma nōn placet. _____

   _____

   _____

4. *Discipulī* **quī** semper **student** ā grammaticō laudantur. _____

   _____

   _____

5. Nōs *lapidibus* **quī cadēbant** paene percussī sumus. _____

   _____

   _____

6. "Quid est nōmen," rogat Cornēlia, "*adulēscentis* **quī** hūc **venit**?" _____

   _____

   _____

7. Cornēlius cum *servō* **quī** epistulam **affert** diū loquitur. _____

   _____

   _____

8. Nēmō *incendium* **quod** incolās **opprimit** exstinguere potest. _____

   _____

   _____

9. Grammaticus *discipulōs* **quī** in lūdō **dormiunt** vehementer castīgābit. ____

   _____

   _____

10. Praedōnēs *cīvibus* **quī** nocte per Subūram **ambulant** pecūniam adiment. __

   _____

   _____

   _____

Activity 41b

Fill in the blanks with Latin words to match the English cues:

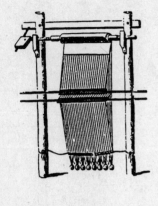

1. Cornēlia _____ multās hōrās _____ . (fabric) (had woven)

2. Sextus nōn satis _____ lūdō habet. (of enthusiasm)

3. "_____ discere," inquit Sextus, "mihi nōn placet." (Such things)

4. "_____ tē dēlectābit," inquit Aurēlia, "Valerium vidēre!" (How much...!)

5. Cornēlius _____ ā Cūriā sextā hōrā _____ . (is said) (to have departed)

6. Līberī _____ sine custōde _____ _____ nōn solent. (in Rome) (to go outside)

7. Puerī patrem ad _____ magnum _____ cōnspexērunt. (temple) (going forward)

8. "Nūllās habeō," inquit Cornēlia, "amīcās in urbe _____ ." (living)

9. Cornēlia fābulam dē servō Valerium ē perīculīs _____ audīre valdē cupiēbat. (rescuing)

10. Valerius in Bīthȳniā _____ _____ aberat, sed Rōmam _____ _____ regrediētur. (for many years) (in a few months)

Activity 41c

Translate into English. Then underline each participle in the Latin sentences and draw lines from the participles to the nouns that they modify:

1. Flāvia cum Cornēliā Rōmam regrediente īre nōn poterat.

   _____

   _____

2. Flāvia, sōla in cubiculō sedēns, dē amīcā suā optimā cōgitābat.

   _____

   _____

3. "Quandō," sēcum cōgitābat, "Cornēliam rūrsus vidēbō?"

   _____

4. "Quantum eam dēsīderō!"

   _____

5. Eō ipsō tempore patrem cum mātre in ātriō loquentem audīvit.

   _____

   _____

6. Flāvia quam celerrimē ē cubiculō ēgressa in ātrium intrāvit.

   _____

   _____

7. Cum prīmum parentēs cōnspexit, "Pater māterque," inquit, "Baiīs diūtius morātī sumus. Licetne nōbīs Rōmam īre?"

_____

_____

8. Pater Flāviae rogantī respondit sīc: "Fortasse, parvula. Epistulam ad Cornēlium mittam."

_____

_____

9. "Sī ille nōs invītāverit, illūc ībimus."

_____

Activity 41d

1. **Give the Latin verb to which the noun** *studium, -ī, n.,* **is related:**

   _____

2. **For each definition below, give an English word derived from** *studium:*

   a. to pursue knowledge by reading, investigating, and contemplating:

   _____

   b. devoted to the pursuit of knowledge, dedicated to learning:

   _____

   c. an artist's workroom: _____

   d. one who attends an educational institution: _____

CHAPTER 42 | A SLAVE TO THE RESCUE

Activity 42a

Give the imperfect and pluperfect subjunctive active of the following verbs in the 3rd person singular:

Imperfect Subjunctive Active	Pluperfect Subjunctive Active
1. obsideō, obsidēre, obsēdī	
2. dēleō, dēlēre, dēlēvī	
3. percutiō, percutere, percussī	
4. adimō, adimere, adēmī	
5. dēsiliō, dēsilīre, dēsiluī	
6. discō, discere, didicī	
7. condō, condere, condidī	
8. poscō, poscere, poposcī	
9. iaciō, iacere, iēcī	
10. compleō, complēre, complēvī	

Activity 42b

Read the following story:

A Beauty Contest

Dī deaeque omnēs ad nūptiās vocātī erant. Pēleus enim, quamquam mortālis erat, deam quandam, Thetim nōmine, uxōrem dūcēbat. Sōla tamen ē dīs immortālibus Discordia nōn invītāta erat, cum molesta deīs cēterīs semper esset. Sī dī rixābantur, sī hominēs rixābantur, illa gaudēbat.

Cum omnēs nūptiās celebrārent laetī, subitō Discordia, īrāta quod nōn invītāta erat, ingressa, mālum aureum in mediōs hospitēs iēcit. Dī deaeque nōn iam bibēbant, nōn iam saltābant; mālum pulcherrimum diū spectābant. Tandem Iuppiter, rēx deōrum, "Litterae," inquit, "in eō scrīptae sunt."

Minerva rogāvit quae litterae in eō essent.

"Dētur pulcherrimae!" respondit Iuppiter.

"Meum igitur est," clāmāvit Venus.

"Minimē!" exclāmāvit Iūnō. "Meum est."

"Nēmō," interpellāvit Minerva, "pulchrior est quam ego."

Mox omnēs rixābantur. Subitō, "Tacēte, omnēs!" clāmāvit Iuppiter. "Nōlīte rixārī! Paris, fīlius Priamī, rēgis Troiānōrum, iūdex erit et mālum pulcherrimae ē vōbīs dabit, nam vir sapientissimus est."

Itaque Mercurius trēs illās deās ad Paridem dūcere iussus est. Ubi advēnērunt, Mercurius,

"Ō Paris," inquit, "et Iūnō et Minerva et Venus volunt id mālum habēre in quō est scrīptum 'dētur pulcherrimae.' Iuppiter tē iūdicem ēlēgit quod eī sapientissimus esse vidēris."

Paris, quamquam difficile erat iūdicāre quis esset pulcherrima, laetus tamen erat quod Iuppiter eum hoc facere iusserat. Trēs deae Paridī placēre valdē cupiēbant.

Iūnō prīma, "Sī mē ēlēgeris," inquit, "ego tibi dabō rēgnum maximum atque tū eris rēx clārissimus."

Minerva secunda, "Sī mē ēlēgeris, glōriam aeternam habēbis. Mīles praeclārus eris."

Ultima Venus, "Sī mē ēlēgeris, fēminam omnium pulcherrimam uxōrem dūcēs." Et Venus Paridī persuāsit.

nūptiae, -ārum, f. pl., *wedding*
rixor, -ārī, -ātus sum, *to quarrel*
aureus, -a, -um, *golden*
dētur, *let it be given*
iūdex, iūdicis, m., *judge*
sapiēns, sapientis, *wise*
ēligō, ēligere, ēlēgī, ēlēctus, *to choose*

Activity 42c

In the story in Activity 42b, find a *cum* causal clause, a *cum* circumstantial clause, and two indirect questions. Translate the sentences in which they occur:

Cum causal clause:

_____

_____

Cum circumstantial clause:

_____

_____

Indirect questions:

_____

_____

_____

Activity 42d

From the story in Exercise 42b, copy all subordinate clauses of the following types that have their verbs in the indicative:

Concessive (introduced by **quamquam**):

_____

_____

Conditional (introduced by **sī**):

_____

_____

_____

Causal (introduced by **quod**):

_____

_____

_____

Temporal (introduced by **ubi**):

_____

VOCABULARY FOR REVIEW

NOUNS

1st Declension

Aenēās, Aenēae, m., *Aeneas (son of Venus and Anchises and legendary ancestor of the Romans)*

Āfrica, -ae, f., *Africa*

Athēnae, -ārum, f. pl., *Athens*

Bīthȳnia, -ae, f., *Bithynia (province in Asia Minor)*

casa, -ae, f., *hut, cottage*

Cremōna, -ae, f., *Cremona (town in northern Italy)*

Crēta, -ae, f., *Crete (large island southeast of Greece)*

ferula, -ae, f., *cane*

Gallia, -ae, f., *Gaul*

Hesperia, -ae, f., *Hesperia (the land in the West, Italy)*

Hispānia, -ae, f., *Spain*

īrācundia, -ae, f., *irritability, bad temper*

Ithaca, -ae, f., *Ithaca (island home of Ulysses)*

lingua, -ae, f., *tongue, language*

litterae, -ārum, f. pl., *letter, epistle, letters, literature*

Mantua, -ae, f., *Mantua (town in northern Italy)*

ōra, -ae, f., *shore*

poena, -ae, f., *punishment, penalty*
poenās dare, *to pay the penalty, be punished*

rēgīna, -ae, f. *queen*

ruīna, -ae, f., *collapse, ruin*

scapha, -ae, f., *small boat*

Sicilia, -ae, f., *Sicily*

tēla, -ae, f., *web, fabric*

terra, -ae, f., *earth, ground, land*

Thrācia, -ae, f., *Thrace (country northeast of Greece)*

Troia, -ae, f., *Troy*

unda, -ae, f., *wave*

2nd Declension

altum, -ī, n., *the deep, the sea*

annus, -ī, m., *year*

arma, -ōrum, n. pl., *arms, weapons*

Augustus, -ī, m., *Augustus (first Roman emperor)*

bellum, -ī, n., *war*

Dēlos, -ī, f., *Delos (small island off the eastern coast of Greece)*

deus, -ī, nom. pl., **dī,** dat., abl. pl., **dīs,** m., *god*

discipulus, -ī, m., *pupil*

fātum, -ī, n., *fate*

fundus, -ī, m., *farm*

Horātius, -ī, m., *Horace (Roman poet)*

Latium, -ī, n., *Latium (the area of central Italy that included Rome)*

magister, magistrī, m., *schoolmaster, master, captain*

Mediolānum, -ī, n., *Milan*

oppidum, -ī, n., *town*

Pompeiī, -ōrum, m. pl., *Pompeii*

respōnsum, -ī, n., *reply*

studium, -ī, n., *enthusiasm, study*

superī, -ōrum, m. pl., *the gods above*

templum, -ī, n., *temple*

torus, -ī, m., *couch*

ventus, -ī, m., *wind*

verbum, -ī, n., *word, verb*

3rd Declension

Aenēis, Aenēidis, f., *the Aeneid (an epic poem by Vergil)*

Alpēs, Alpium, f. pl., *the Alps*

Carthāgō, Carthāginis, f., *Carthage (city on the northern coast of Africa)*

comes, comitis, m./f., *companion*

Dīdō, Dīdōnis, f., *Dido (queen of Carthage)*

dolor, dolōris, m., *grief*

genus, generis, n., *race, stock, nation*

hiems, hiemis, f., *winter*

Iūnō, Iūnōnis, f., *Juno (queen of the gods)*

lītus, lītoris, n., *shore*

mare, maris, abl. sing., **marī,** gen. pl., **marium,** n., *sea*

mēnsis, mēnsis, m., *month*

moenia, moenium, n. pl., *city walls*

nāvis, nāvis, gen. pl, **nāvium,** f., *ship*

ōs, ōris, n., *mouth, face, expression*

procācitās, procācitātis, f., *insolence*

pūgiō, pūgiōnis, m., *dagger*

rogātiō, rogātiōnis, f., *question*

rūs, rūris, n., *country, country estate*
rūre, *from the country*
rūrī, *in the country*
rūs, *to the country*

sōlitūdō, sōlitūdinis, f., *solitude*

tempestās, tempestātis, f., *storm*

Ulixēs, Ulixis, m., *Ulysses, Odysseus (Greek hero of the Trojan War)*

valētūdō, valētūdinis, f., *health (good or bad)*

4th Declension

domus, -ūs, f., *home*
domī, *at home*
domō, *from home*
domum, *homeward, home*

ADJECTIVES

1st and 2nd Declension

abōminandus, -a, -um, *detestable, horrible*

aeger, aegra, aegrum, *ill*

Albānus, -a, -um, *of Alba Longa (city founded by Aeneas' son, Ascanius)*

aliquī, -ae, -a, *some*

altus, -a, -um, *tall, high, deep*

armātus, -a, -um, *armed*

īnfandus, -a, -um, *unspeakable*

intentus, -a, -um, *intent, eager*

īrācundus, -a, -um, *irritable, in a bad mood*

Latīnus, -a, -um, *Latin*

Lāvīnius, -a, -um, *of Lavinium (name of town where the Trojans first settled in Italy)*

profugus, -a, -um, *exiled, fugitive*

saevus, -a, -um, *fierce, savage*
territus, -a, -um, *frightened*
vērus, -a, -um, *true*

3rd Declension
crūdēlis, -is, -e, *cruel*
dīves, dīvitis, *rich*
memor, memoris, *remembering, mindful, unforgetting*
pauper, pauperis, *poor*
rediēns, redeuntis, *returning*
septentriōnālis, -is, -e, *northern*
tālis, -is, -e, *such, like this, of this kind*
tālia, tālium, n. pl., *such things*
terribilis, -is, -e, *frightening*

NUMBERS
Cardinal
ūnus, -a, -um, *one*
duo, duae, duo, *two*
trēs, trēs, tria, *three*
quattuor, *four*
quīnque, *five*
sex, *six*
septem, *seven*
octō, *eight*
novem, *nine*
decem, *ten*
ūndecim, *eleven*
duodecim, *twelve*
tredecim, *thirteen*
quattuordecim, *fourteen*
quīndecim, *fifteen*
sēdecim, *sixteen*
septendecim, *seventeen*
duodēvīgintī, *eighteen*
ūndēvīgintī, *nineteen*
vīgintī, *twenty*
quīnquāgintā, *fifty*
centum, *a hundred*
quīngentī, -ae, -a, *five hundred*
mīlle, *a thousand*

Ordinal
prīmus, -a, -um, *first*
secundus, -a, -um, *second*
tertius, -a, -um, *third*
quārtus, -a, -um, *fourth*
quīntus, -a, -um, *fifth*
sextus, -a, -um, *sixth*
septimus, -a, -um, *seventh*
octāvus, -a, -um, *eighth*
nōnus, -a, -um, *ninth*
decimus, -a, -um, *tenth*
ūndecimus, -a, -um, *eleventh*
duodecimus, -a, -um, *twelfth*
tertius decimus, -a, -um, *thirteenth*
quārtus decimus, -a, -um, *fourteenth*
quīntus decimus, -a, -um, *fifteenth*
sextus decimus, -a, -um, *sixteenth*
septimus decimus, -a, -um, *seventeenth*
duodēvīcēsimus, -a, -um, *eighteenth*
ūndēvīcēsimus, -a, -um, *nineteenth*
vīcēsimus, -a, -um, *twentieth*
quīnquāgēsimus, -a, -um, *fiftieth*
centēsimus, -a, -um, *hundredth*
quīngentēsimus, -a, -um, *five-hundredth*
mīllēsimus, -a, -um, *thousandth*

VERBS
1st Conjugation
aegrōtō, -āre, -āvī, -ātūrus, *to be ill*
dormitō, -āre, -āvī, *to be sleepy*
iactō, -āre, -āvī, -ātus, *to toss about, drive to and fro*
ignōrō, -āre, -āvī, -ātus, *to be ignorant, not to know*
migrō, -āre, -āvī, -ātūrus, *to move one's home*
natō, -āre, -āvī, -ātūrus, *to swim*
nāvigō, -āre, -āvī, -ātus, *to sail*
obsecrō, -āre, -āvī, -ātus, *to beseech, beg*
recitō, -āre, -āvī, -ātus, *to recite*
renovō, -āre, -āvī, -ātus, *to renew, revive*
superō, -āre, -āvī, -ātus, *to overcome*

2nd Conjugation
dēleō, dēlēre, dēlēvī, dēlētus, *to destroy*
moneō, -ēre, -uī, -itus, *to advise, warn*
obsideō, obsidēre, obsēdī, obsessus, *to besiege*
pāreō, -ēre, -uī + dat., *to obey*
studeō, -ēre, -uī + dat., *to study*
valeō, -ēre, -uī, -ītūrus, *to be strong, be well*

3rd Conjugation
animadvertō, animadvertere, animadvertī, animadversus, *to notice*
arcessō, arcessere, arcessīvī, arcessītus, *to summon, send for*
canō, canere, cecinī, cantus, *to sing*
conticēscō, conticēscere, conticuī, *to become silent*
convalēscō, convalēscere, convaluī, *to grow stronger, get well*
discō, discere, didicī, *to learn*
ēvādō, ēvādere, ēvāsī, ēvāsus, *to escape*
expellō, expellere, expulī, expulsus, *to drive out, expel*
extendō, extendere, extendī, extentus, *to hold out*
incendō, incendere, incendī, incēnsus, *to burn, set on fire*
omittō, omittere, omīsī, omissus, *to leave out, omit*
redūcō, redūcere, redūxī, reductus, *to lead back, take back*
repellō, repellere, reppulī, repulsus, *to drive off, drive back*
resistō, resistere, restitī + dat., *to resist*
texō, texere, texuī, textus, *to weave*
vīvō, vīvere, vīxī, vīctūrus, *to live*

3rd Conjugation *-iō*
cupiō, cupere, cupīvī, cupītus, *to desire, want*
rapiō, rapere, rapuī, raptus, *to snatch, seize*

4th Conjugation
dēsiliō, dēsilīre, dēsiluī, *to leap down*
sepeliō, sepelīre, sepelīvī, sepultus, *to bury*

Irregular

īnferō, īnferre, intulī, illātus, *to bring in*

Deponent Verbs
3rd Conjugation

expergīscor, expergīscī, experrēctus sum, *to wake up*

nāscor, nāscī, nātus sum, *to be born*

3rd Conjugation -*iō*

morior, morī, mortuus sum, *to die*

patior, patī, passus sum, *to suffer, endure*

4th Conjugation

adorior, adorīrī, adortus sum, *to attack*

coorior, coorīrī, coortus sum, *to rise up, arise*

ōrdior, ōrdīrī, orsus sum, *to begin*

Semi-deponent Verbs

audeō, audēre, ausus sum + infin., *to dare*

gaudeō, gaudēre, gāvīsus sum, *to be glad, rejoice*

leō, solēre, solitus sum + infin., *to be accustomed (to), be in the habit of*

PREPOSITIONS

ante + acc., *before, in front of*

ob + acc., *on account of*

post + acc., *after*

trāns + acc., *across*

ADVERBS

abhinc, *back from this point in time, ago*

ante, *previously, before*

clam, *secretly*

forās, *outside*

immō vērō, *on the contrary, in fact*

inde, *from there, then*

interdum, *from time to time*

nusquam, *nowhere*

post, *after(ward)*

prīmō, *first, at first*

quam prīmum, *as soon as possible*

Quantum...! *How much...!*

sīc, *thus, in this way*

CONJUNCTIONS

antequam, *before*

cum, *when, since*

cum prīmum, *as soon as*

quoniam, *since*

INTERROGATIVE WORDS AND PHRASES

Quot...? *How many...?*

Quotus, -a, -um, *Which (in numerical order) . . . ?*

MISCELLANEOUS

Avē!/Avēte! *Hail! Greetings!*

coepī, *I began*

dīcitur, *he/she/it is said*

īdem ac, *the same as*

interest, *it is important*

multīs post annīs, *many years afterward*

neque...neque...quidquam, *neither...nor...anything*

Prō dī immortālēs! *Good heavens!*

recitandī, *of reciting*

vēra dīcere, *to tell the truth*

Activity IXa

Translate into Latin, using participles wherever possible:

1. Setting out before dawn tomorrow, we will go to Tusculum; after a few days we will return to Rome.

2. The Cornelii were not able to stay in their country house near Baiae the whole summer.

3. Do you wish to set out from Rome with me in three days, Titus?

4. Having stayed in Carthage a short time, Aeneas departed and sailed to Italy.

5. Two of the slaves who were getting the carriage ready were carrying chests.

6. The boys saw a building standing near the road.

7. Thieves were concealing themselves in the building standing near the road.

8. The name of the building standing near the road was the Flavian Amphitheater.

9. The thieves attacked the boys who were approaching the building.

10. The boys, when attacked, fled home as quickly as possible.

Activity IXb

ACROSS

1. daring (nom. pl.)
4. returning
9. so
10. 1500
12. four
14. great (masc.)
16. nothing
17. which (fem. abl. sing.)
18. he was born
21. well
25. that (fem. nom. sing.)
26. from Brundisium
27. his, her, its
31. in seven years
33. it is important
36. the rest (neut. nom. pl.)
39. him
40. rich
41. he will set on fire
42. his own (abl. pl.)
43. one thousand
44. napkins

DOWN

2. at that time
3. I am
5. ninth (masc.)
6. kitchen
7. through
8. to pay the penalty
11. rather careful
13. you drive
15. her own (fem. abl. sing.)
18. not even
19. you are
20. I have learned
22. she was going
23. I eat
24. this (neut. abl.)
29. to have fallen
30. pig
32. please
34. from Troy
35. hurray
37. who (masc. nom. pl.)
38. in the winter
39. them (dat.)
40. while
42. if

PART 1
PLANNING A JOURNEY

Activity 1a

Translate:

1   Cornēlius cum familiā iam diū Rōmae erat. A.d. IV Nōnās Augustās, Cornēlius multās
2 hōrās in Forō occupātus erat. Vesperī Marcus et Sextus in ātriō lūdēbant cum intrāvit
3 Cornēlius.
4   "Crās," inquit, "amīcum vīsitāre dēbeō. Tusculī haud longē ab urbe Rōmā habitat.
5 Quattuor post diēbus Rōmam regrediar. Vīsne mēcum venīre, Marce? Sextus quoque
6 nōbīscum veniet, nisi molestus fuerit."
7   Rogāvit Marcus, "In raedā iter faciēmus, pater?"
8   Cui respondit pater, "Minimē vērō! Māter tua nōbīscum venīre nōn vult. Itaque in
9 raedā iter nōn faciēmus. Servōs iubēbō equōs parāre. Equīs nōs Tusculum portābimur. Ita
10 ad vīllam amīcī celeriter adveniēmus."
11   Eō tempore tamen Cornēlia in ātrium intrāvit.
12   "Quid audiō?" inquit. "Ad vīllam amīcī iter facere in animō habēs, pater? Cūr nōn mē
13 eō tēcum dūcēs?"
14   At Sextus, "Puellae semper sunt molestae. Cūr nōn domī cum mātre tuā manēs,
15 Cornēlia? Semper tū nōbīscum venīre vīs."
16   Cornēlius tamen, "Tacē, Sexte!" inquit. "Sī Cornēlia nōbīscum venīre vult, licet. Servōs
17 iubēbō raedam extrā portam Caelimontānam parāre. Crās māne abībimus. Ante noctem ad
18 vīllam pervenīre in animō habeō. In caupōnā iterum pernoctāre nōlō."

4 **haud,** adv., *not*

17 **Caelimontānus, -a,
-um,** *at the Caelian
Hill*

**porta Caelimontāna,
-ae,** f., *the Porta
Caelimontana*

Activity 1b: Prepositional Phrases

Locate fifteen different prepositional phrases in the reading passage and copy them here:

_____

_____

_____

Activity 1c: Prepositional Phrases

Underline the correct word or phrase and translate:

1. Cornēlius in (Forō/Forum) occupātus erat.

_____

2. Ad (vīllam/vīllā) per (Viae Appiae/Viam Appiam) crās ībimus.

_____

3. Interdiū intrā (urbem/urbe) raedās agere nōn licet.

_____

4. Vīlla amīcī Cornēliī est prope (Tusculō/Tusculum) nōn procul ā (montem pulchrum/monte pulchrō).

_____

_____

5. Ad (portā/portam) vīllae iānitor dormiet.

_____

6. "Nārrā mihi dē (vīllā/vīllam) amīcī tuī," inquit Cornēlia.

_____

7. "Vīlla sita est inter (duōs montēs/duōbus montibus)," inquit Cornēlius, "et nōn est sine (aquam optimam/aquā optimā)."

_____

_____

8. Quam diū apud (amīcō tuō/amīcum tuum) manēbimus?" rogat Cornēlia.

_____

9. "Paucīs diēbus ē (vīllā/vīllam) ēgrediēmur et Rōmam reveniēmus."

_____

Activity 1d: Irregular Verbs

1. Locate two occurrences of forms of the verb *nōlō* in the reading passage in Activity 1a.

_____

2. Locate three occurrences of forms of the verb *volō* in the reading passage in Activity 1a.

_____

Activity 1e: Irregular Verbs

Change the main verb in each of the following sentences from singular to plural or from plural to singular, keeping the same person, number, and tense. Make other changes as necessary.

1. Nōlō hodiē ad vīllam īre.

_____

2. Crās puella ad vīllam īre nōlet.

_____

3. Heri ad vīllam īre nōlēbātis.

_____

4. Heri ad vīllam ībāmus.

_____

5. Ad vīllam īre hodiē nōn potes.

_____

6. Puella ad vīllam hodiē nōn it.

_____

7. Nōlīte īre hodiē!

_____

8. Crās ad vīllam ī!

_____

9. Estisne dēfessī?

_____

10. Servī, ferte cistās ad raedam!

_____

11. Cistās ad raedam fers.

_____

12. Servī cistās ad raedam ferunt.

_____

13. Equī poterunt nōs ad vīllam ferre.

_____

14. Crās poterō ad vīllam īre.

_____

15. Crās erō Tusculī.

_____

16. Herī erās Rōmae.

_____

17. Crās ad vīllam īre volēs.

_____

18. Crās ad vīllam nōn ībō.

_____

19. Hodiē ad vīllam īre volō.

_____

20. Heri ad vīllam īre poterat.

_____

21. Hodiē ad vīllam īre nōn vīs.

_____

Activity 1f: Place Clues
Using the reading passage in Activity 1a as a guide, give the Latin for:

1. in (or at) Rome _____
2. in the Forum _____
3. from the city (of) Rome _____
4. in Tusculum _____
5. to Rome _____

6. to Tusculum _____
7. to the country house _____
8. into the atrium _____
9. at home _____
10. in the atrium _____

Activity 1g: Place Clues
Give the Latin for the phrases in italics in the following sentences:

1. They were going *to Brundisium*. _____
2. They stayed *at Brundisium*. _____
3. After three days he went away *from Brundisium*. _____
4. We will return *home* in the summer. _____
5. Flavia lives *in a neighboring country house*. _____
6. Tomorrow we will depart *from Rome*. _____
7. After three days we will return *to Rome*. _____
8. We will spend the whole summer *at Baiae*. _____
9. Next summer we will return *to Baiae*. _____
10. Cornelius and his family were *at home in Rome* for a long time. _____

Activity 1h: Time Clues
Using the reading passage in Activity 1a as a guide, give the Latin for:

1. for a long time now _____
2. for many hours _____
3. in the evening _____

4. four days later _____
5. at that moment (time) _____
6. before night(fall) _____

Activity 1i: Time Clues
Give the Latin for the italicized phrases in the following sentences:

1. *Three days later* we will return to Rome.

   _____

2. Cornelius was occupied in the Forum *for five hours*.

   _____

3. *Before the third hour* Cornelius was already tired.

   _____

4. *In three hours* he will depart for Tusculum.

   _____

5. Cornelius arrived at the Forum *three hours ago*.

   _____

6. *At that very moment (time)* he was not tired.

   _____

PART 2
HEADING FOR TUSCULUM

Activity 2a
Translate:

Postrīdiē raeda ā servīs parāta erat extrā Portam Caelimontānam. Ibi servī cum raedā 1
Cornēlium līberōsque exspectābant. 2

Prīmā lūce Cornēlius lectīcās condūxit et cūnctī celeriter portam petīvērunt. Dum per 3
viās cīvium servōrumque hūc illūc concursantium plēnās ībant, templa ingentia et aedificia 4
ēlegantissima urbis admīrābantur. Mox ad Portam Caelimontānam pervēnērunt. In raedam 5
ascendērunt. Iam per Viam Tusculānam profectī sunt. Puerī servōs in agrīs et vīneīs 6
labōrantēs viatōrēsque in viā ambulantēs spectābant. Cornēlia tamen dormiēbat quod diēs 7
iam erat calidior. 8

Subitō raedārius puerīs clāmāvit, "Puerī, spectāte! Ecce, mīlitēs!" Puerī laetī Cornēliam 9
excitāvērunt. Cornēlia īrācunda mīlitēs spectāvit quī iter per viam celeriter faciēbant. Nunc 10
dormīre nōn poterat. 11

Itaque, "Sī iter est longum, pater," inquit, "cūr nōn fābulam nōbīs nārrās? Fābulam dē 12
puellā nōbīs nārrā! Illās fābulās nōn amō quae dē virīs fortibus nārrantur. Nōnne fābulam 13
dē puellā praeclārissimā celeberrimāque nārrāre potes?" 14

"Nūllae sunt puellae praeclārissimae," Cornēliae Sextus inquit. 15

Sed Marcus, "Eucleidēs mihi fābulam dē Atalantā nūper nārrāvit—" 16

Sextus procācī cum rīsū interpellāvit, "Dē puellā quae nōmen tam rīdiculum habēbat 17
audīre nōlō. Dē rēbus iocōsīs audīre volō." 18

Marcus tamen, "Sī soror mea dē Atalantā audīre vult, mihi placet. Dē Atalantā, pater, 19
nōbīs nārrā!" 20

_____

_____

_____

_____

_____

_____

_____

_____

_____

_____

_____

_____

_____

_____

Activity 2b: Nouns

Match each noun at the left (taken from the designated line in the reading passage in Activity 2a) first with its case and then with its use within the phrase or sentence in which it occurs:

1. lūce (3) _____ _____
2. cīvium (4) _____ _____
3. urbis (5) _____ _____
4. raedam (5) _____ _____
5. viātōrēs (7) _____ _____
6. diēs (7) _____ _____
7. puerīs (9) _____ _____
8. iter (10) _____ _____
9. pater (12) _____ _____
10. rīsū (17) _____ _____
11. nōmen (17) _____ _____

A. Nominative
B. Genitive
C. Dative
D. Accusative
E. Ablative
F. Vocative

a. subject
b. direct object
c. with intransitive verb
d. with preposition
e. time
f. possession
g. direct address
h. manner
i. with adjective

Activity 2c: Nouns

1. In the reading passage in Activity 2a, locate in sequence one noun of each declension. Copy the nouns into the spaces below in the forms in which they appear in the passage. Identify the gender, case, and number of each noun:

1st: _____ _____

2nd: _____ _____

3rd: _____ _____

4th: _____ _____

5th: _____ _____

2. On separate sheets of paper write all of the forms *(Nom., Gen., Dat., Acc., Abl., Voc., singular and plural)* of the five nouns you located in 1 above.

Activity 2d: Adjectives

The following adjectives are taken from the designated lines of the reading passage in Activity 2a. For each adjective give the corresponding positive or comparative or superlative forms. Be sure your new forms agree with the noun that the adjective modifies:

Positive	*Comparative*	*Superlative*
1. ingentia (4)	_____	_____
2. _____	calidior (8)	_____
3. īrācunda (10)	_____	_____
4. fortibus (13)	_____	_____
5. _____	_____	praeclārissimā (14)
_____	_____	celeberrimā (14)
6. _____	_____	praeclārissimae (15)
7. procācī (17)	_____	_____
8. rīdiculum (17)	_____	_____
9. iocōsīs (18)	_____	_____

Activity 2e: Adjectives

1. Give the comparative and superlative of each of the following adjectives:

bonus, -a, -um   _____   _____

magnus, -a, -um   _____   _____

malus, -a, -um   _____   _____

parvus, -a, -um   _____   _____

2. Give an English word derived from each comparative and superlative form that you wrote above and give the meaning of each English derivative:

_____   _____

_____   _____

_____   _____

_____   _____

_____   _____

_____   _____

_____   _____

_____   _____

Activity 2f: Present Infinitives

Locate in the reading passages in Activities 1a and 2a one example of a present infinitive used with each of the following verbs or phrases. Translate the sentence in which each occurs:

1. dēbeō (1a:4)

_____   _____

2. volō (1a:5)

_____   _____

3. nōlō (1a:18)

_____   _____

4. iubeō (1a:9)

_____   _____

5. in animō habeō (1a:12)

_____   _____

6. possum (2a:11)

_____   _____

Activity 2g: Present Passive Infinitives

Change each of the following infinitives to the passive, and translate the passive form:

1. amāre   _____   _____

2. monēre   _____   _____

3. expellō   _____   _____

4. excipere   _____   _____

5. pūnīre   _____   _____

PART 3
ATALANTA

Activity 3a
Translate:

Pater hanc fābulam nārrāre coepit.	1
Ōlim in Graeciā habitābat puella quaedam pulcherrima, nōmine Atalanta. Multī virī	2
eam uxōrem dūcere volēbant. Atalanta tamen, quod celerrimē currere poterat, omnibus	3
virīs, "Sī tū celerius quam ego cucurreris," inquit, "ego uxor tua erō. Sī tamen ā mē victus	4
eris, tū statim necāberis."	5
Dūrae certē erant eae condiciōnēs, sed multī currere volēbant. Ūnus, deinde alius	6
fortūnam temptābat. Ēheu! Quamquam multī cucurrērunt, omnēs victī sunt; poenās	7
dedērunt omnēs.	8
Inter spectātōrēs autem ōlim erat adulēscēns quīdam, nōmine Hippomenēs, quī, cum	9
prīmum Atalantam vīdit, statim amāvit. Itaque, quamquam perīculōsissimum erat, currere	10
cōnstituit. Amīcī eum retinēre nōn poterant. Eīs, "Ego," inquit, "Atalantam vincere	11
possum. Venus, quae amantibus favet, mihi auxilium dabit." Deam igitur auxilium rogāvit;	12
illa eī tria māla aurea dedit et, "Hīs bene ūtere," inquit.	13
Diē cōnstitūtā et adulēscēns et puella summā celeritāte currēbant. Hippomenēs, quod	14
Atalanta prīmum locum iam sūmpserat, prīmum deinde secundum ē tribus mālīs ante	15
puellam currentem iēcit. "Haec quidem māla," sēcum cōgitābat, "puellam ā cursū āvertent."	16
Illa bis mālum petīvit. Ille bis puellam praeteriit. Sed Atalanta, ubi clāmōrēs	17
spectātōrum audīvit, multō celerius cucurrit. Hippomenem praeteriit atque fīnī cursūs iam	18
appropinquābat. At Hippomenēs, "Nunc, ō dea," inquit, "fer mihi auxilium!" Tum tertium	19
mālum longē iēcit. Dum puella hoc mālum petit, Hippomenēs ad finem cursūs pervēnit.	20
Victa est puella. Victor laetus ab cursū puellam dūxit.	21

---

6 dūrus, -a, -um, *harsh*

13 ūtōr, ūtī, ūsus sum + abl., *to use*

14 diē cōnstitūtā, *on the appointed day*

16 cursus, -ūs, m., *race*

16 āvertō, āvertere, āvertī, āversus, *to turn away*

17 bis, adv., *twice*

_____

_____

_____

_____

_____

_____

_____

_____

_____

_____

_____

_____

_____

_____

_____

_____

_____

_____

_____

_____

Activity 3b: Numbers

1. **Answer the following questions in Latin:**

   Quot māla Venus virō dedit?

   _____

   Quotum mālum Hippomenēs longē iēcit?

   _____

2. **Give the cardinal numbers in Latin from one to twelve and an English derivative of each of the first ten:**

   _____   _____

   _____   _____

   _____   _____

   _____   _(English: quadr-)_

   _____   _____

   _____   _____

   _____   _____

   _____   _____

   _____   _____

   _____   _____

   _____

   _____

3. **Fill in the blanks with the corresponding Arabic ordinals (the first is done for you):**

_6th_	sextus	_____	nōnus
_____	quārtus	_____	prīmus
_____	duodecimus	_____	septimus
_____	secundus	_____	mīllēsimus
_____	centēsimus	_____	vīcēsimus
_____	octāvus	_____	decimus
_____	ūndecimus	_____	quīntus
_____	quīnquāgēsimus	_____	quīngentēsimus
_____	tertius	_____	duodēvīcēsimus

Activity 3c: Pronouns and Demonstrative Adjectives

1. **In the reading passage in Activity 3a, locate in sequence pronouns that mean:**

her	_____	him	_____	these	_____
you	_____	to them	_____	she	_____
I	_____	to me	_____	he	_____
me	_____	to him	_____		

2. In each of lines 1, 6, 16, and 20 of the reading passage in Activity 3a, locate a demonstrative adjective and the noun that it modifies. Give the gender, case, and number of each adjective-noun combination.

Line 1: _____

Line 6: _____

Line 16: _____

Line 20: _____

3. Fill in the forms on the following charts:

Singular

	Masc.	*Fem.*	*Neut.*	*Masc.*	*Fem.*	*Neut.*	*Masc.*	*Fem.*	*Neut.*
Nom.	is	ea	id	hic	haec	hoc	ille	illa	illud
Gen.	____	____	____	____	____	____	____	____	____
Dat.	____	____	____	____	____	____	____	____	____
Acc.	____	____	____	____	____	____	____	____	____
Abl.	____	____	____	____	____	____	____	____	____

Plural

Nom.	____	____	____	____	____	____	____	____	____
Gen.	____	____	____	____	____	____	____	____	____
Dat.	____	____	____	____	____	____	____	____	____
Acc.	____	____	____	____	____	____	____	____	____
Abl.	____	____	____	____	____	____	____	____	____

4. In lines 9 and 12 of the reading passage in Activity 3a, locate two relative pronouns. Identify the antecedent of each. Then explain the gender, number, and case of each relative pronoun.

Relative pronoun: _____ . Antecedent: _____ .

Gender and number and why: _____

_____

Case and why: _____

_____

Relative pronoun: _____ . Antecedent: _____ .

Gender and number and why: _____

_____

Case and why: _____

_____

5. Fill in the correct forms of the relative pronoun in the following sentences:

a. Virī, _____ Atalanta vīcit, necātī sunt. (whom)

b. Condiciōnēs, _____ Atalanta imposuit, dūrae erant. (which)

c. Multī, _____ cucurrērunt, victī sunt. (who)

d. Vir, _____ amīcī retinēre nōn poterant, erat Hippomenēs. (whom)

e. Hippomenēs, _____ Venus māla dedit, Atalantam vincere poterat. (to whom)

f. Māla, _____ Venus virō dedit, erant aurea. (which)

g. Spectātōrum clāmōrēs, _____ Atalanta incitāta est, erant magnī. (by which)

h. Mālum, _____ Hippomenēs longē iēcit, erat tertium. (which)

i. Atalanta, _____ Hippomenēs uxōrem dūxit, erat laeta. (whom)

Activity 3d: Adverbs

1. In line 20 of the reading passage in Activity 3a, locate a positive adverb ending in -ē: _____

   In lines 3 and 4, locate a superlative and a comperative adverb: _____

2. Give the positive, comparative, and superlative adverbs made from each of the following adjectives:

	Positive	Comparative	Superlative
fēlīx	_____	_____	_____
malus	_____	_____	_____
longus	_____	_____	_____
magnus	_____	_____	_____
dīligēns	_____	_____	_____
bonus	_____	_____	_____
brevis	_____	_____	_____
multus	_____	_____	_____

Activity 3e: Active and Passive Verbs

1. In lines 4–5 of the reading passage in Activity 3a, locate two passive verbs and identify their tenses:

   _____

   _____

   In line 7, locate one passive verb and identify its tense:

   _____

   In line 21, locate one passive verb and identify its tense:

   _____

2. Identify and explain the gender of any perfect passive participles used in the verb forms located in 1 above.

   _____

   _____

   _____

3. Fill in the following chart with the forms of the verb *dūcō*, in the 2nd person singular. Translate each form you give:

	Active	*Passive*
Present	_____	_____
Imperfect	_____	_____
Future	_____	_____
Perfect	_____	_____
Pluperfect	_____	_____
Future Perfect	_____	_____

On separate sheets of paper write out the active and passive forms of the following verbs in all tenses and translate each form you write:

neco: 2nd person pl.
retineō: 1st person pl.
iaciō: 3rd person pl.
audiō: 3rd person sing.

Activity 3f: Imperatives

1. In the reading passage in Activity 3a, locate one imperative in line 13 and one in line 19: _____

2. Give the positive and negative imperatives, singular and plural, for the following verbs:

		Positive	*Negative*
neco	Sing.	_____	_____
	Pl.	_____	_____
retineō	Sing.	_____	_____
	Pl.	_____	_____
dūcō	Sing.	_____	_____
	Pl.	_____	_____
iaciō	Sing.	_____	_____
	Pl.	_____	_____
audiō	Sing.	_____	_____
	Pl.	_____	_____
esse	Sing.	_____	_____
	Pl.	_____	_____
īre	Sing.	_____	_____
	Pl.	_____	_____
ferre	Sing.	_____	_____
	Pl.	_____	_____

PART 4
CLOELIA

Activity 4a
Translate:

1 Līberī patrem fābulam dē Atalantā nārrantem tacitī audīvērunt. Cum is fīnem fēcisset,
2 "Pater," inquit Cornēlia, "nōnne puella Rōmāna quaedam sē fortissimam praebuit?"
3 "Ita vērō, mea parvula!" respondit Cornēlius. "Nōmen illīus puellae erat Cloelia.
4 Cloelia et amīcae eius obsidēs ad castra Porsennae, rēgis Etruriae, quī Rōmam obsidēbat,
5 missae sunt. Eā nocte puellae erant trīstissimae. Lacrimantēs in castrīs sedēbant.
6 "'Quōmodo umquam ex hīs castrīs incolumēs ēvādēmus?' inquiunt. 'Quōmodo Rōmam
7 regrediēmur? Neque patrēs neque mātrēs umquam posthāc vidēbimus?' Tandem,
8 postquam multa tālia inter sē dīxērunt, obdormīvērunt.
9 "Māne tamen Cloelia, quae ad mediam noctem vigilāverat, cōnsilium audāx cēterīs
10 puellīs explicāvit.
11 "'Hodiē,' inquit, 'cum advesperāverit, ē castrīs clam exīre cōnābimur. Necesse erit
12 custōdēs fūrtim vītāre et trāns Tiberim natāre. Nōn difficile erit ita Rōmam pervenīre. Ego
13 nihil vereor; vōs quoque nōlīte verērī.'
14 "Vesperī igitur tacitae ē castrīs ēgressae in aquam dēsiluērunt. Subitō tamen custōdēs,
15 cum sonitum aquae audīvissent, ad rīpam flūminis celeriter dēcurrērunt et puellās
16 cōnspexērunt. Multās hastās in eās iēcērunt. Puellae tamen celeriter natantēs ad alteram
17 rīpam Tiberis incolumēs advēnērunt.
18 "Porsenna, cum audīvisset puellās effūgisse, īrā commōtus nūntiōs statim Rōmam mīsit.
19 "'Nisi hās obsidēs remīseritis,' inquiunt, 'urbem incendēmus.' Itaque Rōmānī invītī
20 puellās remīsērunt. Cum puellae in castra redīssent, Lars Porsenna, 'Obsidibus,' inquit,
21 'nōn licet ē castrīs ēgredī. Itaque vōs reprehendō quod ē castrīs aufūgistis. Sed vōs laudō
22 quod rem tam perīculōsam fēcistis, quamquam puellae modo estis. Itaque vōs Rōmam ad
23 parentēs remittam.'
24 "Tum Rōmānī nōn modo fortitūdinem puellārum laudābant sed etiam in Viā Sacrā
25 statuam puellae equō īnsidentis posuērunt."
26 Cum Cornēlius fīnem fābulae ita faceret, Tusculum advēnērunt.

2 **praebeō, -ēre, -uī, -itus,** *to show*

4 **obses, obsidis,** m./f., *hostage*

7 **posthāc,** adv., *after this, again*

15 **rīpa, -ae,** f., *bank*
flūmen, flūminis, n., *river*

16 **hasta, -ae,** f., *spear*

25 **īnsideō, īnsidēre, īnsēdī, īnsessus** + dat., *to sit on*

_____
_____
_____
_____
_____
_____
_____
_____
_____
_____
_____
_____
_____
_____
_____
_____
_____

_____

_____

_____

_____

_____

_____

_____

_____

_____

_____

Activity 4b: Participles

1. In the reading passage in Activity 4a, locate four present active participles (lines 1, 5, 16, and 25). Identify the gender, case, and number of each participle. Locate the noun that each participle modifies.

   Participle: _____

       Gender, case, and number: _____

       Noun participle modifies: _____

   Participle: _____

       Gender, case, and number: _____

       Noun participle modifies: _____

   Participle: _____

       Gender, case, and number: _____

       Noun participle modifies: _____

   Participle: _____

       Gender, case, and number: _____

       Noun participle modifies: _____

2. In the reading passage in Activity 4a, locate and then identify the gender, case, and number of the following:

   a. a perfect passive participle used as part of a perfect passive verb form (line 5):

   _____

   b. a perfect participle of a deponent verb (line 14): _____

3. Is the perfect participle of a deponent verb (e.g., the participle located in 2.b above) active or passive in form? _____ in meaning? _____

4. Look at the sentences in the reading passage in which the four present active participles that you identified in 1 above occur. Make sure that your translation of these sentences shows that the action described by the present participle was taking place at the same time as the action of the main verb.

5. Look at the sentence in the reading passage in which the perfect participle that you identified in 2b occurs. Make sure that your translation of this sentence shows that the action described by the perfect participle took place prior to the action of the main verb.

Activity 4c: Perfect Active Infinitives

1. Locate one perfect active infinitive in line 18 of the reading passage in
   Activity 4a: _____

2. Give the perfect active infinitives of the following verbs:

accipiō _____ afferō _____ conticēscō _____

dormiō _____ percutiō _____ nārrō _____

scindō _____ ōbsideō _____ cupiō _____

poscō _____ possum _____ resistō _____

parō _____ condō _____ veniō _____

volō _____

Activity 4d: Deponent Verbs

1. In the reading passage in Activity 4a, locate three deponent verbs in the 1st
   person singular or plural (lines 7, 11, and 13): _____

2. In the reading passage in Activity 4a, locate two infinitives of deponent verbs
   (lines 13 and 21): _____

3. Think of active verbs that are approximate synonyms of the deponent verbs
   located in 1 and 2 above, and write the forms of these verbs corresponding to the
   forms of the deponent verbs in the sentences: _____

4. Fill in the following chart with the forms of the verb *loquor*, in the 2nd person
   singular. Translate each form you give:

Present _____

Imperfect _____

Future _____

Perfect _____

Pluperfect _____

Future Perfect _____

On separate sheets of paper write out the forms of the following deponent verbs
in all tenses and translate each form you write:

moror: 2nd person pl.   regredior: 3rd person pl.
vereor: 1st person pl.   experior: 3rd person sing.

Give the positive and negative imperatives, singular and plural, for the following
verbs:

		Positive	*Negative*
moror	Sing.	_____	_____
	Pl.	_____	_____
vereor	Sing.	_____	_____
	Pl.	_____	_____
loquor	Sing.	_____	_____
	Pl.	_____	_____
regredior	Sing.	_____	_____
	Pl.	_____	_____
experior	Sing.	_____	_____
	Pl.	_____	_____

Activity 4e: Subordinate Clauses

1. In the reading passage in Activity 4a, locate subordinate clauses that are introduced by the following subordinating conjunctions and relative pronouns, which are listed in the sequence in which they appear in the passage. Underline each subordinate clause in the Latin story and in your English translation of it:

cum	postquam	cum	cum	cum	quod
quī	quae	cum	nisi	quod	quamquam

2. Give English meanings for the following subordinating conjunctions that you have met but that do not appear in the reading passage in Activity 4a:

dum: _____ or _____   sī: _____

nam: _____   ubi: _____ or _____

Translate the following sentences:

Dum raeda per viam ībat, puerī rūsticōs et agrōs spectābant. Dum puerī aedificia in Forō īnspiciunt, Cornēlium ē Cūriā ēgredientem cōnspexērunt.

_____

_____

_____

Using the reading passage in Activity 4a as a guide, give the Latin for:

a. While the girls were swimming across the Tiber, a guard caught sight of them.

_____

b. As long as the girls were swimming across the Tiber, the guards were throwing spears at them.

_____

3. The subordinate clauses introduced by *cum* in lines 1–2, 11, 15, 18, and 20 of the reading passage in Activity 4a have their verbs in the subjunctive. In all of these clauses but one the word *cum* is best translated *when*. In which clause could you translate it *since* or *because*? Copy that clause here:

_____

4. Translate the following sentences containing subordinate clauses with their verbs in the subjunctive:

a. Sextus nesciēbat quid Cloelia fēcisset.

_____

b. Cornēlius sciēbat quid esset nōmen puellae fortissimae.

_____

c. Cum obsidēs castra Porsennae intrāvissent, diū lacrimābant.

_____

d. Cum mīlitēs castra dīligenter custōdīrent, puellīs necesse erat ē castrīs fūrtim effugere.

_____

_____

e. Cum puellae effūgissent, Porsenna magnā īrā commōtus erat.

_____

This new edition of ECCE ROMANI now offers:

- ◆ beautifully illustrated, full-color, easy-to-read pages
- ◆ color-coded grammar presentations
- ◆ discussion of multiculturalism within the Roman empire
- ◆ consolidated grammar and syntax back matter for easy reference
- ◆ full English to Latin vocabulary at the end of each book
- ◆ annotated Teacher's Guides

The full ECCE ROMANI program is available in a flexible format and includes:

Hardcover Student Book I (I-A and I-B)	0-8013-1201-9
Student Book II (II-A and II-B)	0-8013-1202-7
Student Book III	0-8013-1203-5
Softcover Student Book I-A	0-8013-1204-3
Student Book I-B	0-8013-1205-1
Student Book II-A	0-8013-1206-X
Student Book II-B	0-8013-1207-8
Student Book III	0-8013-1208-6

Teacher's Guide I (I-A and I-B)	0-8013-1217-5
Teacher's Guide II (II-A and II-B)	0-8013-1218-3
Teacher's Guide III	0-8013-1219-1
Language Activity Book I-A	0-8013-1209-4
Language Activity Book I-B	0-8013-1210-8
Language Activity Book II-A	0-8013-1211-6
Language Activity Book II-B	0-8013-1212-4
Teacher's Language Activity Book I-A	0-8013-1213-2
Teacher's Language Activity Book I-B	0-8013-1214-0
Teacher's Language Activity Book II-A	0-8013-1215-9
Teacher's Language Activity Book II-B	0-8013-1216-7

Test Masters Level I (I-A and I-B inclusive)	0-8013-1220-5
Test Masters Level II (II-A and II-B inclusive)	0-8013-1221-3
Test Masters Level III	0-8013-1222-1

Longman

9 780801 312113

90000>

ISBN 0-8013-1211-6

79735